FIRST CHESS OPENINGS

A GREAT BOOK FOR CHESS WINNERS!

T0001796

FIRST CHESS OPENINGS

A GREAT BOOK FOR CHESS WINNERS!

CARDOZA PUBLISHING

ERIC SCHILLER

ACKNOWLEDGMENTS

The author wishes to thank all the proofers who volunteered their time. The following are the names of the proofers who contributed enough to merit personal thanks. In no particular order:

Martin Moller Pedersen
Scott Raevsky
Steve Wolkind
Juliana Ung
Carl Palmateer
Mark Sturman
Ray Bennet
Grahame Booth
James Burden
Peter Tamburro
Marc van Hal

ISBN: 978-1-58042-388-5

Visit our website for a full list of Cardoza Publishing
books and advanced strategies.
CARDOZA PUBLISHING
www.cardozapublishing.com

CONTENTS

INTRODUCTION

First Chess Openings shows you how to confidently start a chess game with solid, near-foolproof openings that will help you win. Inside these easy-to-read pages, you'll find large diagrams, clear explanations, and ideas and concepts that will improve your game. No knowledge of chess notation is required, nor do you need to memorize variations. You'll learn the most important openings, plus the four goals you should accomplish in the early moves of every game of chess. This base of knowledge will take your overall game to the next level—and make playing more fun!

Understanding and employing strong openings is among the most difficult challenges facing new players. Once upon a time, keeping up with opening strategies was easy, as players used only a select group of openings. In the computer age, however, many previously discarded openings have been rediscovered, making this task far more daunting.

If you've struggled to establish strong positions in your first few moves, the lessons in this book will change that. Unlike most books on openings, which often run several hundred pages long, here you will find only the essential elements needed to get you on your way.

The opening strategies presented here have been used by some of the world's finest professional players, but they do not require a great deal of memorization. From the vast palette of opening colors, I have selected the best and brightest, so that the amount of material you will have to absorb is not overwhelming.

This one-of-a-kind book is your first step in mastering the game of chess!

INTRODUCTION TO CHESS NOTATION

ON CHESS NOTATION

Chess moves are written using a special system known as **algebraic chess notation**. Tournament players are required to write down moves of the game using an accepted form of chess notation. Most players use a concise, short form of the notation. This book uses the long form, which is much easier to use. The short form is only used in the graphs. Each move is described using a system of coordinates. The numbers on the left side of the chessboard describe the horizontal rows, called **ranks**. The letters at the bottom indicate the vertical columns, known as **files**.

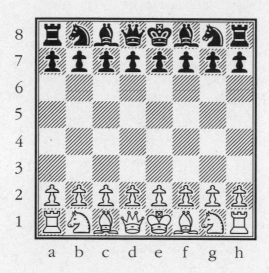

To find the name of a square, you first look at the file, and then find the appropriate rank. In the diagram below, the pawn in the center of the board is at the square e4.

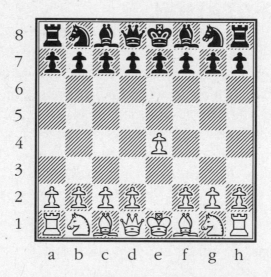

To describe the move that brought the pawn to e4, we indicate both the starting square and landing square, separated by a hyphen or dash: e2-e4. Since this is the first move, we use a move number in front of it:

INTRODUCTION TO CHESS NOTATION

1.e2-e4. That's how we handle normal pawn moves. If something other than a pawn is involved, we include an abbreviation for king (K), queen (Q), bishop (B), knight (N), or rook (R). We have to use "N" for knight, since K is already taken by the king, and the king outranks a knight!

White's move to reach the position shown is 1.Ng1-f3. The knight moved from g1 to f3. The system of describing moves is easy enough, but there are a few wrinkles. If the move is a capture, the starting square and landing square are joined by the letter *x*. If a knight on f3 captures an enemy pawn at e5, we would write it Nf3xe5, not Nf3-e5. If the move puts the enemy king in check it is customary to mark it with a plus sign (+) as a suffix.

If a bishop at c4 captures a pawn at f7, placing the enemy king in check, we use Bc4xf7+. If a pawn advances to the last rank and promotes to another piece, the piece is given after the landing square. If a pawn moved from g7 to g8 and turned into a queen, and the queen places the enemy king in check, then it is g7-g8Q+. Checkmate uses a pound sign (#) instead of a plus sign (+).

Castling has special forms too, generally indicated by connected *O*. If both kingside and queenside castling are possible, you must indicate which it is: O-O is kingside castling, and O-O-O is queenside castling.

FIRST CHESS OPENINGS

Moves are presented in pairs. So 1.e2-e4 e7-e5; 2.Ng1-f3 shows that at the first turn, each player moved the king pawn two squares forward, and then at the second turn, White brought out the knight to f3.

Here is an example of a complete game, the shortest possible checkmate, known appropriately as **Fool's Mate**.

1.g2-g4

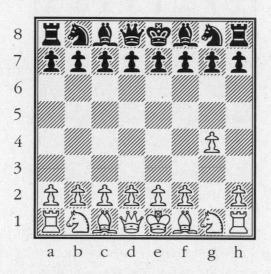

This is without doubt the worst possible opening move. The kingside is weakened, and it won't be safe to castle there. The pawn isn't really attacking anything, and Black can always escape any attack by castling on the queenside

INTRODUCTION TO CHESS NOTATION

1...e7-e5

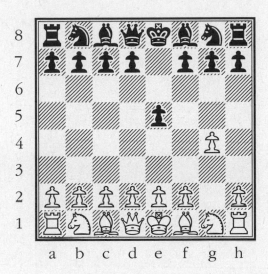

A good reply, planting a pawn in the center and setting up the trap.

2.f2-f4

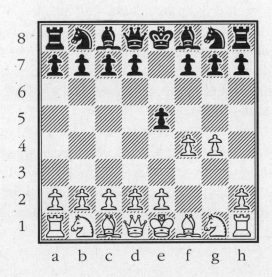

White falls into the trap. The f-pawn should stay home until after you've castled, at least most of the time. The weakness of the king position is fatal!

2...Qd8-h4!#.

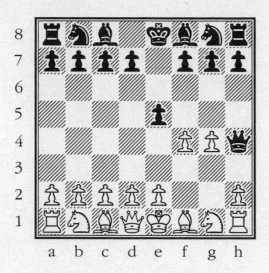

If we want to show Black's move by itself, we use an ellipsis (...), for example Black's checkmating move was 2...Qd8-h4#. The pound sign indicates checkmate.

Notice that above the diagram I have embellished the moves with exclamation and question marks. In this book we will not use a lot of fancy chess symbols. I will award the exclamation mark to moves that I want you to pay particular attention to. These are the moves you should commit to memory. I have marked these moves because they may be too difficult for a beginner to find at the chessboard.

Conventionally, this designation is used to mark moves that are considered the best available moves in the position. In this book, it is used to indicate the best moves for you to use against the level of competition you will ordinarily be facing. You can actually follow all the moves just by moving the piece on the starting square to the indicated landing square. The rest is extra information, included by tradition.

YOUR FIRST CHESS OPENINGS

ON OPENINGS

Many scholastic players invent their own opening strategies or use a preferred stock of moves and formations. They're not concerned with what the chess authorities might think of such moves. Instead, they rely on experience. If an opening strategy works then they are likely to repeat it. If it fails, then they are more likely to switch to some other approach.

Beginners do not play the same openings as the pros. The task is more difficult, because it is not clear at first, whether an opponent's move is good, bad, or simply unusual. I often recommend that players new to the game apply opening strategies from the distant past. Before the twentieth century, opening strategies were, for the most part, quite simple. It was only in the last century that new ideas were introduced to open up a wide variety of strategies based often on ideas that were contrary to popularly held views of the past. It is easier to play like Paul Morphy—the world's best player before the Civil War—than to play like modern superstar Garry Kasparov. Chess in Morphy's day was straightforward and a little bit crude. Modern chess is far more complicated in professional play.

So, for beginners, the best openings tend to be those that were played a long time ago. Such openings are appealing because they are based on simple ideas and strategies that have stood the test of time. This book will teach you how to use these strategies to your advantage, and to understand critical concepts without rote memorization.

Strangely, the openings played by beginners are a lot trickier than those played by professionals. One reason beginning openings are so appealing to novice players is that they contain a great number of dangerous traps. Many seemingly logical moves turn out to be refuted, as most players learn through painful experience. You'll learn to avoid the pitfalls and traps that might lead to a swift and ignominious defeat by following the advice presented in this book.

HOW TO USE THIS BOOK

To get the most out of this book, you need to approach it in the right way, so that it fits your current understanding of the game. If you've been playing for a little while, you should find the amount of material you need to learn reasonable. If you've just learned how to play the game, then you might be a little bit intimidated by all of the different openings and the moves needed for combat.

If you have only learned of the rules of the game, you'll want to pay a lot of attention to the materials in the rest of this chapter. You'll get clear guidelines that will help you to find an acceptable move, even if you don't remember any of the exact moves demonstrated in the book. Above all, you must try to get your king castled to safety. In some openings, this isn't so easy. As you read through the remainder of this book, pay very special attention to those exceptional cases, where you don't get to castle early.

Don't try to memorize a lot of specific variations. Observe the general flow of the opening and in particular remember the moves that are used to get the kingside bishop and knight into the game, so that castling can be achieved. After you have been playing chess for awhile, you'll find that some opening strategies pop up all the time, while most others are rarely or never seen. It is a lot of work to learn all of the openings. Usually, it isn't necessary.

YOUR FIRST CHESS OPENINGS

The openings you really need to know are the ones your opponents choose to play against you. As you encounter opponents who play different openings, you can add these to your arsenal as required. If you have the time, try to learn as many of the opening strategies presented in this book as you can. But don't feel that you have to learn them all in order to be confident at the chessboard.

Charts are presented throughout the book showing the most popular choices for the opposing side. If you are playing against beginners, these statistics won't have much relevance, but as your opposition gets stronger, you will find that the graphs can tell you which moves you are most likely to run into. Rare moves in chess openings tend to be bad moves. You don't have to prepare for them, since you can usually find a good way to counter them during the game, without assistance.

The general guidelines I present should make sure that you don't get into any serious trouble at the start of the game. The specific moves, if you know them, will improve your results. You have to keep in mind that in most cases the opening stage of the game will not be decisive, and results of the game will depend on mistakes made later on. Eventually, you'll become a better chess player. At some point you will want to refine your choice of opening strategies, and take up some more advanced plans. Don't try to change or replace all of your openings at once. Make small changes, adding some deeper knowledge to the openings you already know, or choosing a slightly different path than the one presented in this book.

For example, I recommend the Advance Variation of the Caro-Kann Defense with the move 4.Bd3. Once you have acquired more skills, you might prefer bringing out one of the knights instead of that move. I've kept things as simple as possible. You'll encounter some of these specific opening strategies in later sections.

I believe you can play all of the specific recommendations in this book at least until you are a club-level player. For those familiar with the chess rating system, that would be about 1400 on the ELO scale. You don't need rankings to determine whether your opening strategies are appropriate.

Give yourself some time to gain experience with the suggested moves. Then stick with them as long as you are getting good results. The result of the opening is not the same as the result of the game, of course. Just look at the board after ten moves or so and as long as you are not more than one pawn down, and your king is safe, then the opening is working well enough for you.

THE STARTING POSITION

When you start the game, your pieces are set up according to tradition. Your king is in the center of the board and the army's main forces are sitting behind a row of pawns.

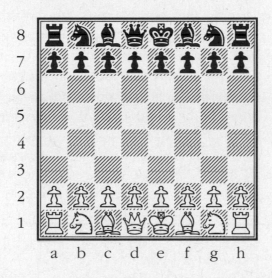

What should you do first? Of course you can simply move pieces as recommended in books or by a teacher, but that's not going to solve the overall problem of getting your pieces into the game. You need to have some idea of what you need to accomplish with your first few moves. I'm going to give you four simple goals. In the main part of this book, I'll be showing you specific moves to use in specific situations, but these goals will allow you to find the best moves, or at least acceptable moves, in every situation.

Your first goal is to take control of part of the center of the board. In most military battles, and a large number of sporting contests, control of the center is a powerful tool in establishing the conditions for successful attack. You should send one or two of your pawns to occupy important central squares. Ideally, you will place pawns both at d4 and e4 as White, or d5 and e5 as Black.

Once we've managed to achieve all or part of this goal, you need to turn your attention to your king. The safety of the king is very important early in the game. Until the king is safe, it is open to attack by enemy forces. To safeguard your king, use the special move known as castling. In order to castle, we must move out all of the pieces that stand between the king and one of the rooks.

It is easiest for the king to castle on the side where there are only two pieces standing between the king and the rook, a bishop and a knight. In the other direction, the queen also would have to be moved. That requires more time, and time is very valuable in the opening.

After you castle, you have to get the rest of your pieces into the game. It is important to consider the role of the rooks. The rooks normally enter the battle from the center of the board, using lines that are opened when some of the central pawns are exchanged. Your third goal is to connect the rooks, by making sure that all of the pieces standing between the rooks are moved out of the way. After castling, of course, the king will already be on the far side of the rooks.

Once your two rooks can see each other, your fourth and final goal is to move one of the rooks onto a central file, either the d-file or the e-file. You can use a file that is open for business. A rook can act only as far as it can see, so sitting right behind a pawn is useless, and should be done only when the pawn absolutely requires the protection of the rook.

THE FOUR GOALS OF OPENINGS

GOAL 1: CREATE IDEAL PAWN CENTERS
GOAL 2: CASTLE!
GOAL 3: CONNECT THE ROOKS
GOAL 4: CENTRALIZE AT LEAST ONE ROOK

We will go through each of these four goals in more detail in the sections that follow. You'll be surprised how effective this opening strategy is. Even if you haven't learned any specific moves, you can avoid trouble by trying to achieve the four goals of openings.

Along the way though, you'll have to watch out for specific threats. You can't just blindly make moves that achieve these goals, while letting your opponent capture all of your pieces!

GOAL 1: CREATE IDEAL PAWN CENTERS

Imagine that your opponent is in a generous mood, and offered you a chance to make the first two moves before replying. You could really take advantage of this by placing two pawns right in the middle of the board.

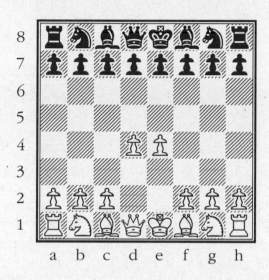

Let's see what we have accomplished. Your two pawns sit in the middle of the board, ready to capture any piece daring to advance to the neighborhood. Both of your bishops can enter the game, your knights can support each of the central pawns, and the queen can come into the game whenever she wants. The only way the king can be attacked is along the diagonal running from a5 to the king's home square at e1. So, your king has a little breathing room, but is not in any danger. Castling can be achieved after just two more moves. Control of the central squares deprives Black of their use. This is illustrated in the picture below, where the controlled squares are highlighted.

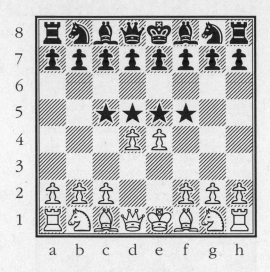

If Black puts any pieces on those highlighted squares, White will be able to capture them. This pretty much limits Black to putting pawns on those squares, and even then the consequences of capturing the pawn would have to be considered.

You can see how putting two pawns in the center of the board leads to good things. In most openings your opponent will not allow you to achieve this. You might be allowed to place the pawns there temporarily, but Black will use something called a **pawn break** to challenge that center. The pawn break takes place when a pawn moves forward to challenge an enemy pawn. In the position above, Black has four potential pawn breaks—one on each of the highlighted squares.

When you're playing with the Black pieces, you will not want your opponent to be able to enjoy the luxury of the ideal pawn center. That's why on the first move, you'll place a pawn in a position to prevent this from happening. You can do so on the very first move, if White moves the king pawn two squares forward. Then you can, and should, move your king pawn two squares forward as well.

If White advances the queen pawn instead, then you should move your queen pawn forward two squares. More advanced players can allow White to establish the ideal pawn center, only to break it down later. However, beginners should stick to the classical method of preventing the ideal pawn center from being established in the first place.

GOAL 2: CASTLE!

Some years ago, I was watching a game being played by one of my top students, a true chess prodigy. His mother was also watching, extremely nervous as always. Her understanding of the game of chess was limited.

As the game went on, her son's king remained on its home square and eventually, it was hunted down. After the game, the mother admonished her son, asking over and over, "Why didn't you castle?" Indeed, this young master, trying to play a sophisticated opening strategy, had left his king in the center far too long, and suffered the consequences.

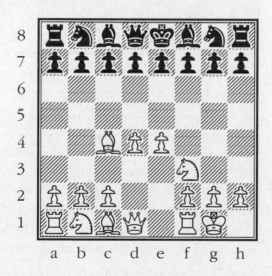

In the made-up position above, we are ignoring Black's moves so we can concentrate on opening strategy for White. You could only achieve such a position if Black were willing to do nothing but move knights out and back to their original squares.

White has set up the ideal pawn center, placed the bishop in an attacking position at c4, and placed the knight on its logical post at f3. With no pieces standing between the king and rook, White was then able to castle.

The castled king is safe, because there are no weaknesses in the pawn barrier standing in front. The knight defends the otherwise weak pawn at the edge of the board. A rook as well as the king guards the always-vulnerable pawn at f2.

You cannot devote all of your attention to keeping your king safe. It would be ridiculous to mobilize your entire army for purely defensive tasks. The castle formation pictured on the previous page is the best way to keep your king safe while giving most of your forces a free hand to go out and inflict damage on enemy positions.

A REMINDER ON CASTLING

The castling rule is a bit tricky, so you have to make sure that you understand how the castling move works, and when you are allowed to use it. Castling was introduced many centuries ago in order to provide a way for each player to get the king to safety early in the game. Castling is a double move, just like the rule that allows you to move a pawn two squares instead of one as long as it is still on its home square.

When you castle, the king makes a double move, moving two squares toward the edge of the board in either direction. The rook then moves to the square on the far side of the king. In tournament competition, it is important to touch the king first, because castling is considered a king move. You can't castle when you're in check, or if the king would be in check after castling, or would be in check on the square it crossed to reach the castled position. In that sense, it is similar to the en passant rule. In that case, a pawn is captured if it moves two squares forward but would have been capturable had it moved only one square. The idea is that whenever you are allowed to make a double move, you aren't allowed to skip past danger.

Either way, many players aren't aware that the restrictions that apply to the king do not apply to the rook. You may castle even when the rook is under attack, or if a square passed over by the rook when castling would make it a target of attack. Castling is a king move, and the restrictions apply only to the king.

GOAL 3: CONNECT THE ROOKS

Once your king is tucked away safely, the next task is to get your pieces into the game. Often, you hear the advice, "develop your pieces." The problem is that they don't say which pieces should be developed. Of course, every situation is a bit different, so it is not always easy to decide how to bring your forces into the game. In any case, you need to involve the rooks at some point. Rooks need room to maneuver, and therefore, you should move out all of the pieces that stand between the rooks. So instead of an abstract notion of developing your pieces, focus on this concrete goal: Let your rooks see each other.

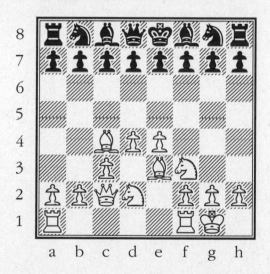

The picture above shows just one possible formation for your pieces. The important thing is that the rooks are connected and either rook can take up a position in the center of the board or wherever it happens to be needed. In this particular case, the queen and bishop and knights are used to support important central squares and only the bishop at c4 is in an attacking position.

There are many other ways of setting up your pieces and, of course, your formation will depend on what the opponent is doing. In this instructional diagram, Black has been doing absolutely nothing so this is not a practical formation. You will notice however, that the White pieces are all in the center of the board, not running around in some far-flung territory, hoping to invade without any real support.

GOAL 4: CENTRALIZE AT LEAST ONE ROOK

Once the rooks are connected it makes sense to move either one or both of the rooks to the center of the board. Keep in mind that the center of the board is where the opening battle of the chess game takes place. Having rooks on the central files makes it possible to launch an early attack against an enemy king, should he remain too long in the center of the board.

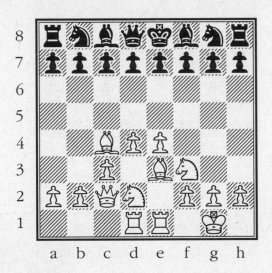

Looking at the formation above, you might think that the rooks are useless, because there are too many pieces in front of them on the central files. This can be deceptive. Pieces standing in the way can often easily be moved out of the way. Pawns are more problematic. However, pawns can get off the highway if any pawn or piece is captured. Since pawns capture diagonally, any capture will remove them from the file they stand on. So rooks and queens can have a powerful influence on a file, even when there are numerous pieces standing in their way.

Once you have brought at least one rook to the center of the board, your opening tasks are complete. Accomplishing the four goals is not always easy. Your opponents will often do things to prevent you from simply seizing the center, castling, and dealing with your rooks. However, once you have completed the four steps, you are ready to engage in the big battles that make up the game of chess.

ON THE VALUE OF THE PIECES

It is very important to know which of your pieces are valuable, and which are expendable. Chess is a very complicated game and the value of pieces is not a fixed number. When starting out in the game, you are often told that each piece is worth a certain amount of points. There is a great deal of disagreement as to what those exact figures are, though generally a pawn is always considered to have a value of one point. Traditionally, knights and bishops are worth three points each, a rook is worth five, and the queen will be either nine or ten points. Using this point system, you can determine whether or not to exchange pieces. For example, two rooks are worth about the same as a queen.

As you gain experience, you'll come to learn that those numbers are very flexible. A lot depends on where the pieces are located and the stage of the game. In the opening part of the game, a pawn is worth next to nothing. Later in the book you'll learn about gambits, openings where a pawn is deliberately sacrificed just so that other pieces can get into the game quickly. In the middle of the game, the value of a pawn depends on where it's located. A pawn guarding your king is obviously worth more than a pawn sitting on the far side of the board. In the endgame, the value of a pawn, which might march all the way across the board and turn into a queen, is much higher.

So don't be surprised when your opponent offers you a pawn or even a knight or bishop in sacrifice. In many cases, the plan will be to recover the sacrifice as quickly as possible. In others, the sacrifice is an investment, used to achieve specific strategic or tactical goals. I have included quite a number of opening strategies that involve sacrifices, so that as you play, you will come to understand a bit of the complicated world of chess pawns and pieces.

YOUR WHITE OPENINGS

ON WHITE OPENINGS

To start the game as White, move your king pawn two squares forward and plant it in the center of the board. This allows you to bring both your bishop and queen into the game, while at the same time, the king remains safe at home.

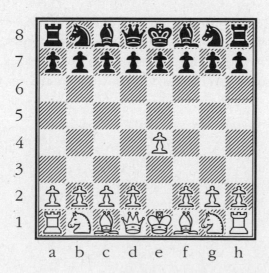

FIRST CHESS OPENINGS

Your next actions depend on what your opponent does in reply to your first move. In most games among beginners, Black responds by moving the king pawn to e5, achieving the same goals as White. In this case, it is already clear that one of your targets will be the weak pawn at f7. As long as the king remains on its home square, that pawn is the cornerstone of Black's defense. In later chapters, you will see how to use your pieces to go after that pawn, even very early in the game.

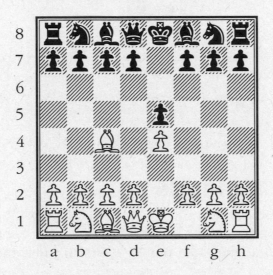

But suppose Black chooses a different first move. For hundreds of years, many players have preferred to move the king pawn one square forward so that the pawn at f7 is not such a juicy target. In this case it would be foolish for you to move your bishop out to the c4 square, as you do when Black chooses to move the king pawn two squares forward on the first move.

YOUR WHITE OPENINGS

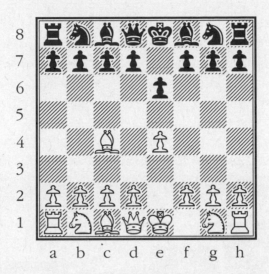

You can see from the diagram above that the bishop would not be very effective when it aims at the well protected pawn at e6. Black's pawn is defended by two other pawns and a bishop is backing them up. There is absolutely no way that you can reasonably expect to make progress against such a formation. So, as you'll see in the chapter on the **French Defense**, which is what this opening is called, you will use a slightly different strategy, not going after the king quite so early in the game.

Black has a choice of twenty moves at the first turn. Each pawn can move either one or two steps forward, and there are four squares available to knights. Fortunately, you do not have to develop a unique strategy for each of these twenty replies. You can reduce the number of strategies you need to less than half a dozen. In most cases, apply the four basic guidelines and you will only have to memorize a few special positions that can arise if your opponent plays the opening recklessly.

In the following chapters, we will go through all of the necessary strategies, relying whenever possible on general principles, and only resorting to memorized moves in certain tricky situations. Before we do that, let's take a look at a chart which shows the moves you are likely to encounter after you move your king pawn forward.

FIRST CHESS OPENINGS

The chart below is based on a collection of chess games played by amateur players, in which White started the game by moving the king pawn two squares forward. This chart—and others throughout the book—reflect what you are likely to encounter, as you progress as a chess player, not necessarily what you are likely to see in games against other beginners or scholastic players.

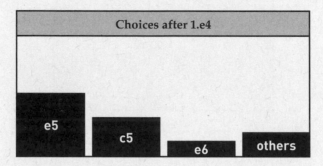

The most popular reply is clearly 1…e7-e5, moving the king pawn forward two squares. From my experience, the next most popular opening in scholastic games is the **Sicilian Defense** (1…c7-c5) because it was the favorite opening of World Champions Bobby Fischer and Garry Kasparov. Then comes the **French Defense** (1…e7-e6), followed by the **Caro-Kann Defense** (1…c6).

All other openings are seen only on very rare occasions. When learning openings you should prepare to meet the most popular openings, while relying on more general principles to deal with uncommon ones.

However, it may be that you have a friend or regular opponent, who enjoys playing one of the lesser-known strategies. In the remaining chapters in this book you'll find the advice for playing against all of the popular openings and a few of the less common openings. The remainder of potential openings don't require any special preparation.

THE MOST COMMON OPENING

1.e2-e4   **e7-e5**

As a beginner, most of your games will start with each king pawn advancing two squares forward. This is the way most students are taught to play the game. A couple of hundred years ago, almost all chess games started this way.

Traditional advice holds that you should bring out your knights before you bring out your bishops. In fact, there is no reason whatsoever to bring out your king's knight before you bring out the king's bishop. By bringing out the bishop first, you can avoid some tricky openings, which require significant preparation to handle properly. So that's what I recommend.

White Attacks with the Bishop

1.e2-e4		e7-e5
2.Bf1-c4		

After you have planted a pawn in the center, it is time to turn your attention to castling. In order to get castled, you must bring out both the bishop from f1 and the knight from g1. Your life will be a lot easier if you bring the bishop out first, because this reduces the number of options available to Black. If you bring the knight out first, you have to contend with the tricky and dangerous **Latvian Gambit** (2…f7-f5) and **Elephant Gambit** (2…d7-d5). Those strategies are not available when you move the bishop to c4 instead.

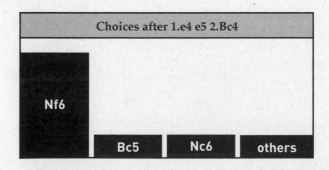

As you can see from the chart, Black has three main defenses. The most popular move by far for Black, is to bring the knight out to f6. Moving the queen's knight to c6 is also a possibility, favored by many players. It is not unusual, especially among beginners, for Black to copy White's moves by bringing the bishop to c5. Minor alternatives for Black include several pawn moves. In each case, you will continue by bringing your knight to f3, so you can castle quickly.

A Tricky Gambit

1.e2-e4	e7-e5
2.Bf1-c4	Ng8-f6

We begin our journey with Black's most popular move, bringing the king's knight into the game at f6. At first, this looks a bit surprising because you are allowing Black to capture your pawn at e4. This strategy is known as a gambit. This particular gambit is known as the **Boden Gambit** after a 19th-century player. You are going to use a refinement of this strategy, seen in the games of the great American player Paul Morphy.

3.Ng1-f3

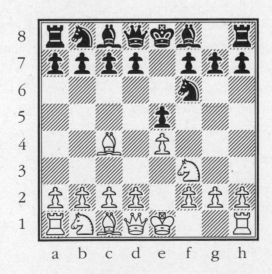

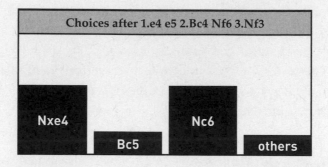

Choices after 1.e4 e5 2.Bc4 Nf6 3.Nf3

You will part with the pawn, temporarily in this case, in order to bring your forces into the game as quickly as possible. Gambits can be effective at all levels of chess, but are found most often in amateur games. Defending against a gambit is difficult and requires solid technique, which of course is usually missing in those new to the game. Professionals are better equipped to deal with gambits, and are rarely caught by surprise.

3...Nf6xe4. If Black does not capture the pawn at e4, then the game will usually reach one of the variations from the next chapters. For 3...Nb8-c6; 4.Nf3-g5, see later sections in this chapter. Make sure you check out 3...Bf8-c5, the Copycat Trap.

4. Nb1-c3. There are many ways to play this gambit. Morphy liked to challenge the enemy knight immediately. Although your general principles suggest you should castle, castling immediately would allow Black to reinforce the knight by advancing the d-pawn to d5. Then your bishop would also be under attack. It is not a good idea to let enemy pieces rest comfortably on your territory, and the enemy knight has, after all, crossed the dividing line and has entered your space.

4...Ne4xc3. Black usually captures the knight, and in fact this move is more popular than all the other replies put together. The obvious alternative is to retreat the knight, and the knight can move backwards to f6 or d6. However, there is also a somewhat tricky line, where Black seems to ignore the threat against the knight at e4, and simply brings out the other knight.

After 4...Nb8-c6, White can capture Black's knight. 5.Nc3xe4 is countered by the surprising resource 5...d7-d5! The pawn at d5, protected by Black's queen on her home square, attacks both your bishop and your knight, so Black will regain the sacrificed piece. Don't fall for this trick. Instead, after Black brings out the queen's knight, simply castle. Then if Black captures your knight at c3, the game will reach positions discussed below, using a different move order.

5.d2xc3.

As a general rule, when two pawn captures are available on the same square, you try to capture toward the center of the board. In this case that would be a poor choice, because in a gambit strategy, where you have already sacrificed one pawn, it is necessary to get your pieces into the game as quickly as possible.

By using the pawn at d2 instead of the pawn at b2, your bishop can emerge from c1 and take up a position on the kingside, for example at g5. More importantly, it allows the bishop to defend one of your other pieces at g5. You would like to move your knight to g5, because then the knight and the bishop can combine forces to attack Black's weak square at f7.

5...f7-f6. Most of the time, Black uses the f-pawn to defend e5, where Black's pawn is under attack. Personally, I do not think that this is the best move but it is the move recommended in most books. There is quite a lot of danger for Black in this position. It is easy to make a bad move, which might even lose the game quickly.

Suppose Black uses the d-pawn instead, advancing it by playing 5...d7-d6? Then after 6.Nf3-g5 Black has an embarrassing problem at f7. In my opinion, Black's best move is 5...c7-c6, followed on the next move by d7-d5, driving back your bishop and depriving it of access to f7. However, in this case you play 6.Nf3xe5, recouping the pawn.

6. O-O.

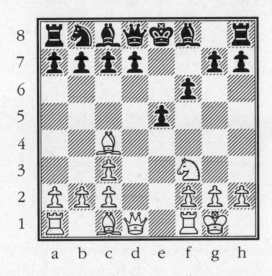

Although you are a pawn down, you have already castled and have two pieces in fighting position. You actually threaten to sacrifice for the pawn at e5 with your knight, since if Black captures it with the pawn at f6, your queen will have a devastating check at h5. You can also set up the same check by moving the knight to h4. There are many interesting traps and tricks from this position, and all of them belong to White! Your king is safe, and your whole army will quickly be mobilized. Black has nothing but two pawn moves to show for his initial efforts.

6…Nb8-c6. If Black defends the pawn at e5 with a pawn at d6, the bishop at f8 has no future.

7.Nf3-h4 g7-g6. Black must defend against the threat of Qd1-h5+, since then it will be too late for the pawn to go to g6, because you can capture the pawn at g6 with your knight. Black's pawn at h7 is pinned to the rook by the queen at h5 and can't safely take the knight. That would give you a pleasant choice between seizing the rook, or taking the pawn with check and going on a king hunt!

8.Rf1-e1.

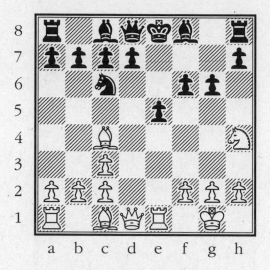

You have a splendid attacking position. You are already castled, with bishop, knight and rook in attacking positions. Black has just one knight in the game, and the kingside pawn structure has already been compromised.

The Traditional Fried Liver Attack: Introduction

1.e2-e4	e7-e5
2.Bf1-c4	Ng8-f6
3.Ng1-f3	Nb8-c6
4.Nf3-g5!	

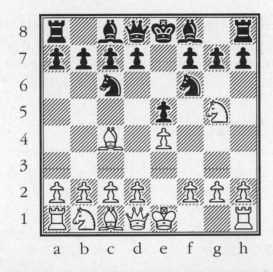

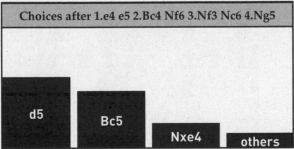

Choices after 1.e4 e5 2.Bc4 Nf6 3.Nf3 Nc6 4.Ng5

Moving the knight to g5 violates the general advice not to move a single piece twice in the opening stage of the game. However, both the knight and the bishop attack Black's weak spot at f7. It is not easy to meet this threat, and even after just a few moves, a fierce battle is raging. Despite its complexity, this strategy for White has been popular for centuries, and is especially common in amateur and scholastic games. Black's most direct defensive plan involves moving the pawn from d7 to d5, attacking the White bishop. There are a few tricky alternatives, and more than any other position in this book, you really need to be prepared for the next few moves. One slip may prove fatal!

Although Black's options are limited to four moves, each poses a challenge to White. You really need to be familiar with each of the replies, or risk a total disaster in the opening. But don't worry, you only need to learn the next two or three moves following Black's response. So pay close attention to what follows, and you'll never fall into the traps. The good news is that you will be assured of an advantage in all cases but one, and even there the chances are reckoned to be equal. That's good news, because after all, you may also be defending this position as Black!

Fried Liver Attack

1.e2-e4	e7-e5
2.Bf1-c4	Ng8-f6
3.Ng1-f3	Nb8-c6
4.Nf3-g5	d7-d5
5.e4xd5	Nf6xd5?!

Capturing the pawn with the knight seems the most logical reply, but you should be very happy when your opponent chooses this path. It usually means that your opponent does not know how to play this opening.

White now has an exciting possibility to sacrifice the knight for the pawn at f7, exposing the Black king to attack. The Black king can be drawn to the center of the board, where it is subject to an all-out assault by White's forces. With extremely precise play, it might be possible for Black to survive. However, in the overwhelming majority of games, Black suffers an early and humiliating defeat.

Because the attack is so much fun, and achieves such tremendous practical results in competition, I recommend that you plunge headfirst into this opening, which is known as the **Fried Liver Attack**. Objectively, White can achieve a superior position by advancing the pawn from d2 to d4, offering it as a gambit.

However, the sacrifice of the knight is more instructive and is the sort of thing every chess player should experience a few times, but only from the White side of the board. Black does not have to allow this strategy, and in the next section, on the Polerio Defense, we'll consider the alternatives.

6.Ng5xf7! Kxf7; 7.Qd1-f3+ Kf7-e6. Black had to capture the knight, which was attacking both the queen at d8 and the rook at h8. In reply to the check by the queen, the king has to move forward to protect the knight at d5. That knight is attacked by both the queen and the bishop and is defended only by the Black queen.

So the king must move into dangerous territory or White will simply recapture the knight. Then White will enjoy the advantage of an extra pawn and still have a strong attack.

8.Nb1-c3. The knight at c3 attacks the enemy knight yet again. The Black knight at d5 is pinned by the bishop at c4 and cannot move. There is only one Black piece in position to come to the aid of its colleague. The knight at c6 must move to either b4 or e7 to protect the knight at d5. Later, the pawn at c6 can advance, to provide additional support.

8...Nc6-e7. If Black moves the knight to b4, you can simply castle, or play more ambitiously, sacrificing your rook by playing 9.a2-a3 Nb4xc2+; 10.Ke1-d1 Nc2xa1; 11.Nc3xd5.

Black has an extra rook, but you threaten to play Nd5xc7, with two simultaneous checks against the Black king, one from the bishop at c4 and the other by the knight at c7. After Black's king retreats, you can then capture the Black rook at a8. If Black plays 11...Ke6-d6, to avoid the discovered check, you can't get the rook back but after you play 12.d2-d4, the enemy king is in serious trouble. You might not beat a computer from this position but most human opponents, especially beginners, won't last long.

So, let's return to the position after 8...Nc6-e7.

This is a less risky defense, but it has the disadvantage of blocking in the bishop at f8. You could castle now, but that gives Black time to breathe, so continue the attack by attacking the brave little pawn defending the king.

9.d2-d4! c7-c6. If Black takes your pawn at d4, you capture the knight at d5 with your knight. Black must recapture with the knight from e7, since using the queen would allow capture by White's bishop. You then bring your queen to e4, giving check. There is no way Black can save the knight at d5. Black's only good move is to defend the knight with the pawn, but you can pile on the pressure.

10.Bc1-g5. You have only one pawn as compensation for your sacrificed knight, but you will be able to castle on either side, and your rooks will attack along the central files.

YOUR WHITE OPENINGS

This is the position you are going to get if Black plays well enough to hold off your opening attack. If Black advances the pawn to h6, to attack your bishop, you capture at e7 and then castle on the queenside.

By castling on the queenside, you gain a rook on the d-file, and can open that line by capturing the pawn at e5 with your pawn at d4. Just aim everything you've got at the enemy king. After all, Black's rooks and bishop at c8 aren't going to be able to help with the defense for a long time. You have your entire army ready to go!

This section contained the most complicated material you need to learn to play effectively as White. You'll have great results if you master this strategy, but even if you make a few mistakes, you will still have excellent chances to attack the exposed king and win the game.

The Officially Approved Defense

1.e2-e4	e7-e5
2.Bf1-c4	Ng8-f6
3.Ng1-f3	Nb8-c6
4.Nf3-g5	d7-d5
5.e4xd5	

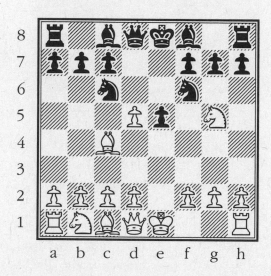

Most of the time your opponent will either capture the pawn at d5, as in the previous section, or move the knight on c6 to a5, which we will look at in a moment. There are, however, additional possibilities that might catch you by surprise, but can be rather tricky.

Suppose Black moves the pawn from b7 to b5 to attack your bishop. That pawn is defenseless, and you can capture it with your bishop, but then the Black queen will capture your pawn at d5. However, you can put your pawn to good use by capturing Black's knight at c6, allowing the Black pawn to capture your bishop at c4.

After the moves **5...b7-b5!?; 6.d5xc6 b5xc4** you play **7.Qd1-e2**. The queen attacks Black's pawns at c4 and e5 and you will be able to quickly castle and bring the rest of your forces into the game.

On the fifth move Black can choose instead to take the knight at c6 out of danger by moving it to d4. You could attack that knight by moving the pawn to c3, but I suggest that you instead, increase the power of your bishop at c4 by advancing your pawn to d6. After **5…Nc6-d4; 6.d5-d6**, Black's pawn at f7 is once again under attack by both your bishop and your knight. On the next move, for your bishop to capture the pawn at f7 after Black's king runs away, you can retreat your bishop back to b3, so that it will be saved. Then you can castle and build your attack.

So, let's now turn your attention to the main line, which has been played thousands of times over the last four hundred years.

>**DEFINITION**
>
>The **main line** is the term used for the most important continuation, the one played the most times by the greatest number of strong players.

>   **5…Nc6-a5!**

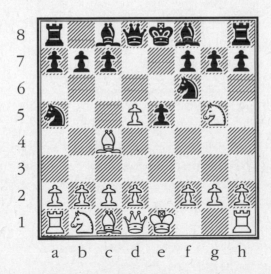

This is Black's best defense, and in fact it is the one you will play, when you are on the Black side of this position. The bishop at c4 is under attack by the knight.

6. Bc4-b5+ c7-c6. This is usually the move played by Black. When you play the Black side of the position you are going to put your bishop at d7 to block the check. If Black tries your strategy, you will play as follows:

6…Bc8-d7; 7.Qd1-e2. Your bishop is defended, and if Black captures your bishop, you can recapture with the queen. At the same time, your queen attacks the undefended pawn at e5. For further discussion of this position, see the section on Two Knights as Black.

7.d5xc6   b7xc6
8.Qd1-f3!?

This is a trap! If Black captures your bishop with the pawn, your queen will swoop down and collect Black's rook at a8! After Black moves, you can retreat your bishop back to e2. Then you will be able to castle.

By the way, if Black should be foolish enough to move the knight at f6, notice that your queen can capture the pawn at f7 with checkmate. This is not a simple position, but it is a lot of fun to play and White's king will be quite safe. Black has to do most of the work.

A Tricky Counterattack

1.e2-e4	e7-e5
2.Bf1-c4	Ng8-f6
3.Ng1-f3	Nb8-c6
4.Nf3-g5	Bf8-c5?!

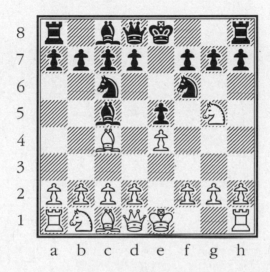

This is Black's trickiest, and most aggressive defense. It isn't entirely sound but to refute it requires a lot of technical knowledge. I recommend a plan which is easy to remember and easy to play. Just grab the pawn at f7 with check, and then get that bishop out of there as fast as you can. So, **5.Bc4xf7+ Ke8-e7; 6.Bf7-b3!**

Don't keep your bishop at f7 when its defender, the knight at g5, can so easily be kicked away. After Black's reply, usually **6...Rh8-f8**, just castle, and then start developing the queenside.

The Wild Line

1.e2-e4	e7-e5
2.Bf1-c4	Ng8-f6
3.Ng1-f3	Nb8-c6
4.Nf3-g5	Nf6xe4

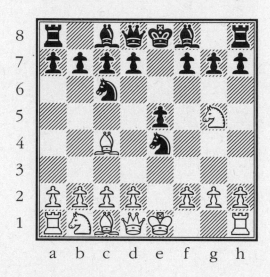

This is a strange move. Black offers you a choice of the pawn at f7 or the knight at e4. You could capture at f7 with the knight, attacking the Black queen and rook with a *fork*, or you might take it with the bishop, forcing the king to move. Or perhaps you should gobble the knight at e4. You can see why Black might try to confuse an opponent with such complications. You should take the pawn with check, so that the enemy king has to move and can no longer castle. After **5.Bc4xf7+ Ke8-e7**, you have a strong move available in **6.d2-d3!**

This not only attacks the enemy knight again, but also cleverly defends your knight at g5. If Black trades knights at g5, you capture with the bishop, putting the enemy king in check. The king can move away, capturing your other bishop in the process, but then you take the queen and come out way ahead.

The Queen Line

1.e2-e4	e7-e5
2.Bf1-c4	Ng8-f6
3.Ng1-f3	Nb8-c6
4.Nf3-g5	Qd8-e7

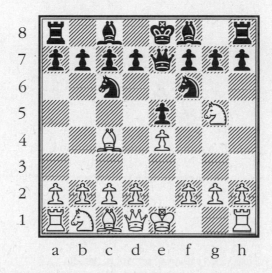

This line is only included because from time to time unskilled players will use it, giving up on the pawn at f7 and getting ready to shift the king to d8. As in the variation where Black chose 4...Bf8-c5 instead of moving the queen to e7, you should capture the pawn with check and get out of town fast. **5.Bc4xf7+ Ke8-d8; 6.Bf7-b3** gives you a very nice game. You can then castle, unless Black overlooks your threat of Ng5-f7+, which forks the king and rook.

Black Brings the Bishop Out Before the Kingside Knight

1.e2-e4	e7-e5
2.Bf1-c4	Bf8-c5
3.Ng1-f3	Nb8-c6
4.O-O	

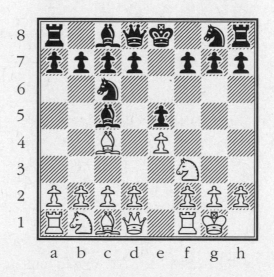

Black sometimes plays 4…d7-d6, hoping to pin your knight with Bc8-g4 on the next move. You can prevent that with 5.h2-h3, taking control of the important g4-square. Normally, Black plays **4…Ng8-f6**, so that castling can come next. You should start getting the queenside into action, with **5.d2-d3**, also protecting your pawn at e4. Then if Black castles, you can pin the enemy knight by moving your bishop to g5. Black can prevent that with **5…h7-h6**, but that gives you time to play **6.c2-c3**, and soon you can advance your pawn to d4 and smash open the center.

Copycat Line

1.e2-e4	e7-e5
2.Bf1-c4	Bf8-c5
3.Ng1-f3	Ng8-f6

We've all played opponents who think they can get away with copying your moves in the opening. Such a strategy is doomed to failure, but White has to be aware of a few little tricks. After you take the pawn with **4.Nf3xe5**, Black usually either castles or recklessly tries to keep the copycat strategy going. 4...Nf6xe4 is a big mistake, because after 5.Bc4xf7+, the king has to move and then White advances the d-pawn to d4, attacking the enemy bishop and eliminating any threats at f2.

After the bishop retreats, you withdraw your own bishop to b3, and hold on to an extra pawn and the right to castle. Black more commonly plays **4...O-O,** getting the king to safety, protecting f7, and preparing to move a rook to the e-file. Still, after **5.d2-d4** the enemy bishop must retreat, since if it moves to b4 with check, you just block by putting a pawn at c3, once again attacking the bishop. On the next move you can defend your e-pawn by pinning the enemy knight, bringing your bishop to g5. Then you can castle.

FRENCH DEFENSE

1.e2-e4	e7-e6
2.d2-d4	

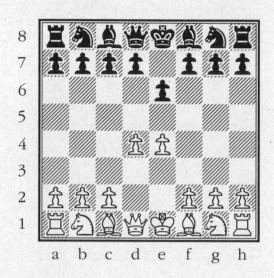

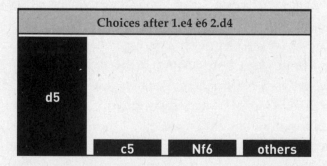

As you can see, Black almost always moves the pawn to d5. That's the idea of the **French Defense**. Rarely, the opponent will try an unorthodox move, such as advancing the pawn to b6 or bringing out the knight to f6. In the first case, just play your knight to f3 and aim for castling. If the knight comes to f6, it attacks your pawn at e4. In this case, push the pawn to e5 and kick the knight. Then aim for castling, and at some point shore up the pawn chain by playing the pawn from c2 to c3.

2...d7-d5; 3.e4-e5.

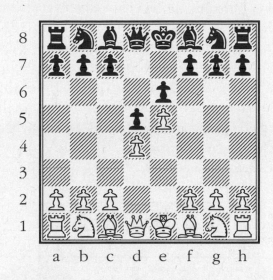

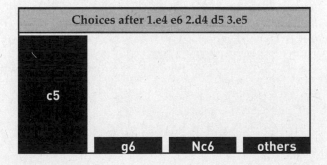

In the French Defense, Black has a strong pawn in the center, but the pawn at e6 locks in the bishop at c8, causing problems that may last for a long time. By advancing your pawn to e5, you ensure that the bishop will remain a prisoner at least throughout the opening phase of the game. This policy of advancing a pawn to e5, with the idea of creating a wall of pawns from the second rank up to e5, will be seen in a number of openings where Black refrains from answering your strategy by placing a Black pawn at e5.

FIRST CHESS OPENINGS

The strategies of this variation of the French Defense have been worked out for centuries. Black will try to undermine your pawn chain, usually by placing pawns at either c5 or f6 or both. White's moves are quite simple, following the plan of bringing out pieces to effective squares and castling early in the game.

We will examine three strategies for Black, starting with the main line and then take a look at some of the exceptional lines that pop up from time to time. However, for the most part, you can play effectively by simply remembering to place a pawn at c3, connecting the links of the pawn chain, developing the kingside pieces and castling. In the overwhelming majority of games, the next few moves are routine.

3...c7-c5; 4.c2-c3 Nb8-c6; 5.Ng1-f3.

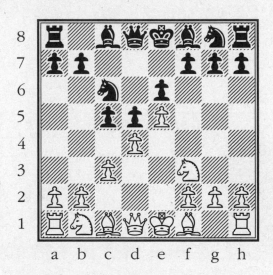

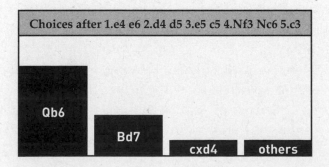

Choices after 1.e4 e6 2.d4 d5 3.e5 c5 4.Nf3 Nc6 5.c3

Qb6

Bd7

cxd4

others

Now it is time for Black to choose a plan. Normally, Black tries to gang up on your pawn at d4. The Black queen can apply pressure at b6. This is just what you are looking for, since you intend to sacrifice that pawn. This strategy is known as the **Milner-Barry Attack**. The plan with 5...Ng8-e7 presents no problems. Just play 6.Bf1-d3 and continue with the usual plan. If the knight goes to f5 to add pressure to the pawn at d4, just capture it. The exchange of bishop for knight will mess up Black's pawn structure.

Attacking the French with a Gambit

1.e2-e4	e7-e6
2.d2-d4	d7-d5
3.e4-e5	c7-c5
4.c2-c3	Nb8-c6
5.Ng1-f3	

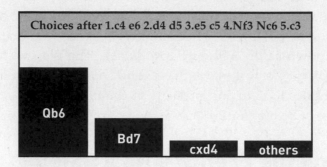

5...Qd8-b6. Black now has two pieces attacking your pawn. The Black pawn at c5 is the immediate aggressor, teaming up with a knight at c6. More fuel can be added to the fire by placing the queen at b6. Your pawn is safely protected by a knight at f3, a pawn at c3, and the queen at d1. Your next move may come as somewhat of a surprise, because by moving your bishop to d3 you reduce your defending force and Black can try to steal the pawn. However, that would be a big mistake, as you'll see.

6.Bf1-d3 c5xd4; 7.c3xd4 Bc8-d7. Why doesn't Black simply capture the pawn with his knight? This is the trap. If Black captures the pawn with the knight (7...Nc6xd4), then White captures the knight (8.Nf3xd4), and if Black takes back with the queen (8...Qb6xd4), White unleashes the stunning move 9.Bd3-b5+. The Black king must deal with the check from the bishop and the White queen will capture the Black queen on the next turn.

By moving the bishop to d7, Black insures that there will not be any inconvenience check on b5 since the diagonal leading to the king is now sufficiently guarded. Now there is a real threat of capturing your pawn at d4, but this is a threat you can ignore.

YOUR WHITE OPENINGS

8.O-O.

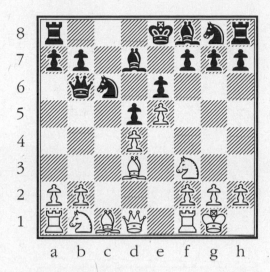

Castling achieves your second opening goal, and it is clear that the rest of your pieces can enter the game quickly. It is true that Black can capture your pawn safely now, but we don't care.

In return for the sacrifice of a pawn, you will rapidly get your pieces into the game and can go after the enemy king, which is stuck in the center. After **8...Nc6xd4; 9.Nf3xd4 Qb6xd4; 10.Nb1-c3**, you offer a second pawn. If Black is brave enough to play **10...Qd4xe5**, then after **11.Rf1-e1** the queen must move away and the pawn at e6 is pinned.

Black can't use the e-pawn to take your knight because it is pinned by the rook, so if the queen retreats to c7, b8, or f6, you can capture the Black pawn at d5 with your knight from c3. If Black doesn't take the pawn at e5, you simply slide your rook to e1 to defend it.

In any case, it is going to take some time for Black to bring forces into the game and safely secure the king. While Black is doing that, you are free to pursue your own goals. Against professional caliber defenders, this strategy might be a bit suspect. In everyday games, however, it is highly effective.

Check Line

1.e2-e4	e7-e6
2.d2-d4	d7-d5
3.e4-e5	c7-c5
4.c2-c3	Nb8-c6
5.Ng1-f3	c5xd4
6.c3xd4	Bf8-b4+

Instead of greedily going after the pawn, Black can choose to develop pieces, for example, bringing the bishop to b4 and putting your king in check. In this case you'll block with the knight.

7.Nb1-c3.

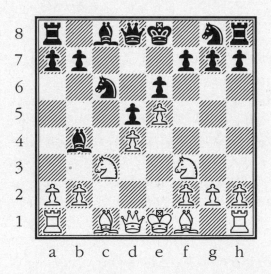

Once you have blocked the check, your strategy remains the same. Following the four guidelines, you are going to move your bishop from f1 to d3, and then castle. After that you can bring out your dark square bishop and slide a rook over to c1. If Black castles on the kingside, as expected, your bishop attacks the crucial square h7.

The attack can be supported by a queen at c2, or you might even retreat your bishop to b1 and then place the queen in attacking position at c2 or d3.

In any case, Black will have a hard time defending against your upcoming onslaught.

Central Challenge

1.e2-e4	e7-e6
2.d2-d4	d7-d5
3.e4-e5	c7-c5
4.c2-c3	Nb8-c6
5.Ng1-f3	f7-f6

This is another way of trying to break up your impressive pawn chain. Black accepts a little weakness on the kingside in return for pressure at e5. You can simply ignore this attack, since the pawn at e5 is secured by a pawn and a knight.

6.Bf1-d3. As usual, you simply develop your bishop and prepare to castle. Black has advanced the pawn from f7 to f6, so the empty square at g6 has become a little bit weaker. This may not seem like much now, but it can have major impact later in the game. Let's take a look at what happens if Black captures the pawn.

6...f6xe5; 7. Nf3xe5.

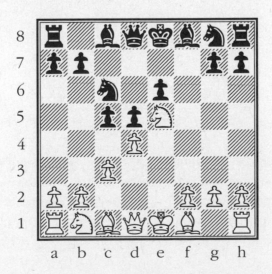

You now have a very strong threat. If Black allows you to move your queen to h5, putting the king in check, Black's pawn can't safely advance to g6 to block the check. If the pawn steps forward, White can sacrifice either the bishop or the knight for that pawn, because Black's pawn at h7 is pinned to the rook. After, for example, 7...Bf8-d6; 8.Qd1-h5+ g7-g6; 9.Bd3xg6+, capturing the bishop with 9...h7xg6 allows 10.Qh5xh8, picking up a rook in exchange for the bishop.

Instead, Black usually plays **7...Ng8-f6**, guarding h5. Then you simply castle, since if Black exchanges knights at e5, you recapture with the pawn and then the knight at f6 has to run away, allowing you access to h5.

SICILIAN DEFENSE

1.e2-e4	c7-c5
2.c2-c3	

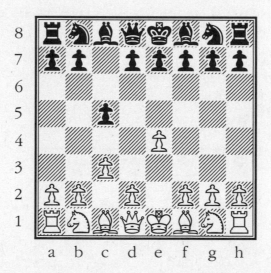

In modern chess, the **Sicilian Defense**, which begins with Black playing a pawn to c5, has become even more popular than the standard **King Pawn Defense**. Some great players, including World Champions Bobby Fischer and Garry Kasparov, have promoted the Sicilian to the extent that it is clearly the most popular defense among professionals. It is also a popular defense among amateur players, though it is not encountered frequently in scholastic games and contests between beginners.

Your response to this opening will be to build a strong pawn center. On your second turn, you advance your pawn from c2 to c3 so that a pawn can later move to d4 with the strong support of the pawn at c3. If Black permits, you may even extend your pawn chain by moving your pawn from e4 to e5. In some cases, the game will transfer to the French Defense, where we also advocate the building of a big pawn chain. This transfer is achieved after the moves 2...e7-e6; 3.d2-d4 d7-d5, reaching the position from the French Defense discussed in the previous chapter.

After you advance the pawn, Black can choose from a number of paths. In most cases, you can more or less ignore Black's moves and simply advance your pawn to d4, followed by bringing out your knight and bishop on the kingside in anticipation of castling.

There are, however, two moves that immediately attack your pawn at e4 and therefore must be dealt with separately. These two plans involve the advance of Black's pawn from d7 to d5 or a Black knight moving from g8 to f6, with play similar to the **Alekhine Defense** (1.e2-e4 Ng8-f6; 2.e4-e5 Nf6-d5).

Black Smashes Open the Center

1.e2-e4	c7-c5
2.c2-c3	d7-d5
3.e4xd5	

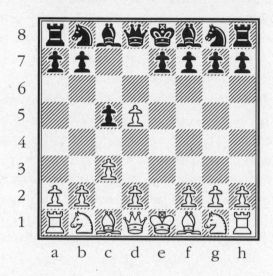

In the Sicilian Defense, Black attempts to play pawn to d5 as soon as possible. When you place your pawn at c3 on the second move, this acts as an invitation for Black to carry out that plan immediately. Indeed, advancing the pawn to d5 on the second move is the most popular response to your move 2.c2-c3.

If you take the pawn at d5, Black can safely recapture with the queen, because your knight cannot go to c3 to attack the queen, since you have a pawn occupying that square. Black is not obliged to recapture the pawn immediately, but can instead bring out a knight to f6 and capture the pawn on the following turn. In either case, the chances are considered approximately level.

Fortunately, this position is very easy to play for White. The next moves will be advancing a pawn to d4, bringing out a knight to f3, putting your bishop at e2, and castling. You don't really need to know very much about the theory of this opening.

Just follow your basic rules, and you'll be fine. A typical line runs **3...Qd8xd5; 4.d2-d4 Ng8-f6; 5.Ng1-f3 Bc8-g4; 6.Bf1-e2 Nb8-c6; 7.O-O**. If Black tries to win the pawn at d4, you can have a knockout punch ready: 7...c5xd4; 8.c3xd4. This creates a weak, isolated pawn at d4. If Black gets greedy and trades the bishop for the knight in order to win that pawn, the result will be disaster. 8...Bg4xf3; 9.Be2xf3 and if 9...Qd5xd4, then you capture the knight at c6 with your bishop, giving check and capturing the enemy queen on the next move.

The Dance of the Knight

1.e2-e4	**c7-c5**
2.c2-c3	**Ng8-f6**
3.e4-e5	**Nf6-d5**
4.d2-d4	

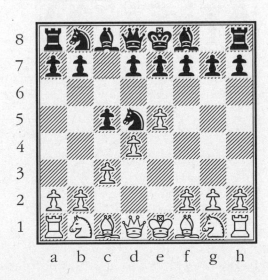

When Black brings the knight out to f6, you can advance the attacked pawn to e5 to kick that knight. After it moves, support the advanced pawn by playing your d-pawn to d4. This creates the same kind of the pawn chain that you use against the French Defense (1...e7-e6), and the Caro-

Kann Defense (1...c7-c6), which is discussed in detail in the next chapter.

This is also a very easy position to handle at the board. Your next moves will be to bring out the knight and bishop on the kingside and get castled. After that you simply follow the general directions for connecting your rooks and moving one to the center and everything will be fine. Here is a typical continuation: **4...c5xd4; 5.c3xd4 Nb8-c6; 6.Ng1-f3 d7-d6; 7.Bf1-c4,** and if Black chases the bishop with **7...Nd5-b6**, move it to b5, where it pins the enemy knight.

THE CARO-KANN DEFENSE

1.e2-e4	c7-c6
2.d2-d4	d7-d5
3.e4-e5	

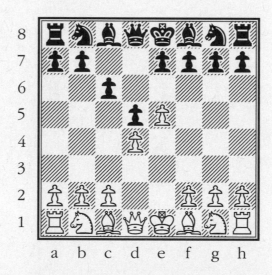

The **Caro-Kann Defense** features a solid central formation with Black's pawn at d5 supported by a colleague at c6. The advantage of the Caro-Kann over the French is that without any pawn on e6 to block the way, the bishop at c8 can quickly get into the game. This opening is usually preferred by players who enjoy a quiet game and dislike flamboyant attacking positions. Your strategy will be to build the pawn chain by advancing your pawn from c2 to c3, bringing out the kingside knight and bishop and castling as usual. Black almost always moves the bishop to f5 on the third move, but there are three minor alternatives.

Black can offer a gambit by advancing the c-pawn, which has just moved from c7 to c6, and moving it one step further to c5. Professionals consider capturing that pawn to be the most effective reply, but it leads to unnecessary complications in the opening.

Instead, you will stick with your main strategy and simply move your pawn from c2 to c3 to defend the pawn at d4. Against the uncommon responses 3...Nb8-a6 and g7-g6, simply bring out your knight to f3 and bring out the bishop and castle. If Black later attacks your d-pawn by advancing to c5, just support the pawn by playing c2-c3. So you should not place your knight on that square.

Against the primary defense, 3...Bc8-f5, White has no less than eight interesting possibilities. To keep things simple, you are going to choose one of the least exciting and least complicated. You are going to offer an immediate exchange of bishops with 4.Bf1-d3.

FIRST CHESS OPENINGS

1.e2-e4	c7-c6
2.d2-d4	d7-d5
3.e4-e5	Bc8-f5
4.Bf1-d3	

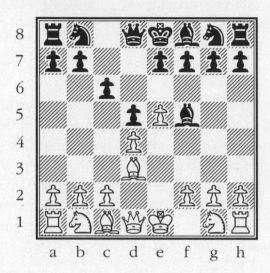

If Black declines your offer to exchange, simply bring your knight out to f3 and then castle. After that you will follow your normal scheme of development: connect your rooks, strengthen the pawn chain by advancing a pawn to c3. Your knight at b1 can enter the game via d2, and your advantage in space will secure a long-term advantage. So let's concentrate on the exchange of bishops.

4...Bf5xd3; 5.Qd1xd3 e7-e6. This is the natural move, allowing the bishop to get into the game from f8. However, it is not easy to find a useful position for that bishop, because it cannot sit comfortably at e7. If the bishop occupies e7 the knight at g8 has no place to go. Black does not want to move the knight to h6, because then it can be captured by White's bishop, shattering the pawn structure on the kingside. You can see that Black already has a problem to solve involving the development of the knight from g8.

6.Ng1-e2. Try to remember to place the knight at e2 in this variation. It won't do much harm if you put your knight at f3 instead, but the knight can be better used at squares like f4 and g3, which are accessible from the station at e2.

Black has many plans from this position, sometimes wrestling the knights into position, sometimes developing the queen on the queenside, and often advancing the pawn from c6 to c5 to challenge your pawn chain. In this last case, the game can continue along paths such as **6...c6-c5; 7.c2-c3 Nb8-c6; 9.O-O**.

Sooner or later Black is going to have to figure out how to get the pieces out and castle. You can bring your knight from the b2 to d2, and later move it to f3 so that both of your knights occupy useful positions. This entire variation is much easier to play as White, and even though professional players might consider the position equal, I expect that in most amateur games, White will prevail.

LIVING ON THE EDGE

The Modern Defenses are characterized by Black's bishop being developed quickly to g7. The idea is not to do battle in the center right away, but to allow White to develop a strong center and then hack away at it from the edges. The game usually develops slowly, with confrontation postponed until the middle game.

1.e2-e4	g7-g6
2.d2-d4	Bf8-g7
3.c2-c3	d7-d6

Since Black is aiming his bishop right at your d-pawn, you'll support it with a pawn. Black's combination of a triangle formation on the kingside, the *fianchetto* with the one-step advance of the d-pawn identifies the opening as the **Modern Defense**.

If instead of 3...d7-d6, Black had chosen 3...c7-c5, then you will soon be in the territory of the Sicilian Defense. If Black had pushed the d-pawn two squares, 3...d7-d5 would be met by the advance 4.e4-e5. Then 4...c7-c6 would bring about your line against the Caro-Kann Defense, while 4...c7-c5 would also lead to your Sicilian lines. Finally, with 3...c7-c6, Black is likely to play d7-d5 on the next move, which transfers the game to the Caro-Kann.

So, from the position in the diagram, you need to bring out your knight and bishop on the kingside, so that you can get castled quickly.

4.Bf1-c4 Ng8-f6; 5.Qd1-e2.

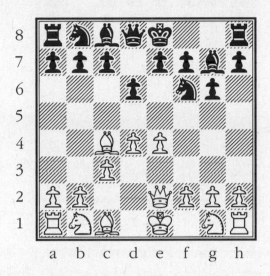

Your pawn at e4 is now defended, and you can play according to general principles. You will bring your knight out to f3, castle, and then find useful squares for your queenside pieces.

DEALING WITH THE FLEXIBLE DEFENSE

1.e2-e4	**d7-d6**
2.d2-d4	**Ng8-f6**

Black can go in many directions after these moves. We can limit the options by directly attacking the f7-square, our favorite target.

3.Bf1-c4

This is a tricky move. You offer the pawn at e4 to the enemy knight. If it is captured, you can recover it using a clever tactic. Black should think twice before accepting the gambit. With 3...g7-g6, planning to fianchetto the bishop at g7, the game will transfer to the position we looked at in the Modern Defense after you move the queen to e2.

Another plan is 3...c7-c6, known as the **Czech Defense**. If Black chooses that, just bring out the knight to c3, to defend the pawn at e4. Then bring out the other knight and get castled. Black might be tempted to stake a claim in the center by moving the pawn to e5, but if that happens, you capture it, and after Black recaptures, you can swap queens, forcing the enemy king recapture. Then Black can't castle. When Black captures the pawn with **3...Nf6xe4**, you unveil the shocking move **4.Bc4xf7+!**

The sacrifice of the bishop is only temporary, you'll get the Black knight soon enough. Black will play **4...Ke8xf7**, of course. Then you bring your queen out with check, **5.Qd1-h5+**.

Black can then block with the g-pawn, retreat the king to g8, or advance it to e6. In the first two cases you move your queen to d5, putting the king in check yet again, and then you'll capture the knight at e4 on the next move. If Black tries to prevent that by playing **5...Kf7-e6**, you can take advantage **6.d4-d5+**, and the only move to counter the check is **6...Ke6-f6**.

If Black didn't have a knight at e4, you could clobber Black by moving your bishop from c1 to g5, checking the king again. The king would have to move up the board to f5 or e5.

Then your bishop goes queen hunting, capturing the pawn at e7. This exposes the Black king to a check from your queen at h5, Black can't prevent the loss of the queen. So, just play **7.Nb1-c3,** and let Black worry about what to do about the threats.

THE LAZY DEFENSE

1.e2-e4   **d7-d5**

This opening, also known as the **Scandinavian Defense**, is often the choice of players who do not want to bother learning many opening lines. Since White is almost certainly going to capture the pawn, it is easy to predict the next few moves.

2.e4xd5.

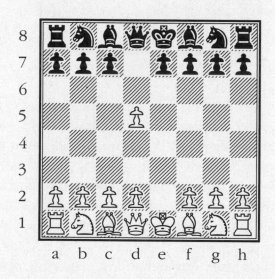

Black immediately confronts your central pawn by advancing the d-pawn to d5. You can—and should—capture this pawn. Black can recapture immediately, with the queen, or delay the capture of the pawn and bring the knight out to f6, so that the knight can capture the pawn. If Black captures immediately with the queen, you will have to resist the temptation to kick her by bringing your knight from b1 to c3.

Instead, advance your pawn from d2 to d4 so that you will have a pawn in the center, as your general guidelines require. Next, calmly bring out your forces, starting with the knight at g1, which will take up its customary position on f3. After that, bring out the bishop from f1 and castle to safety. Here are two typical move sequences showing you how to play the opening.

2...Qd8xd5. We'll focus on the queen capture, which is the most popular move. In the unlikely event your opponent plays 2...Ng8-f6, just play 3.Ng1-f3, then bring out the bishop and castle.

3.d2-d4 Ng8-f6. If Black advances a pawn to c5 or e5 instead, you can capture the pawn. Then if Black swaps queens you enjoy an extra pawn, and if the queen captures either pawn, she'll eventually be attacked by your bishops and knights. For example, 3...e7-e5; 4.d4xe5 Qxe5+; 5.Bg1-e2 followed by Ng1-f3 and castling.

4.Ng1-f3 Bc8-g4; 5.Bf1-e2.

As you can see you are ready to castle and can kick the Black queen by moving your pawn from c2 to c4 or by bringing your knight from b1 to c3. If Black now moves the knight from b8 to b6, it would seem to contain the threat of capturing your knight with the bishop and then capturing your pawn at d4 with the queen.

However, this runs into exactly the same trick that you see in the Sicilian break: **5...Nb8-c6; 6.0-0 Bg4xf3; 7.Be2xf3 Qd5xd4** drops the queen to **8.Bf3xc6+**, since in answer to the check Black must either capture the bishop with 8...b7xc6, allowing 9.Qd1xd4, or retreat the queen to d7, where she will be captured by the bishop.

BLACK ATTACKS YOUR PAWN WITH THE KNIGHT

1.e2-e4   Ng8-f6
2.Bf1-c4

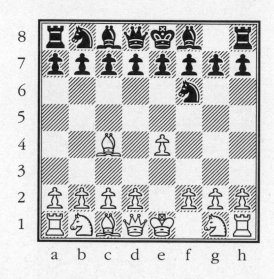

The **Alekhine Defense** is not among Black's more popular plans, and you are rarely likely to encounter it or any of the openings in the following chapters. It is generally recommended that you advance your pawn to e5 to attack the enemy knight, but this requires a solid understanding of the nuances of the Alekhine Defense. Since you're not going to run into it all that often, I propose a simple and easy alternative to remember. This is a fun variation, all the moves are rather forced and many take your opponent by surprise.

The reason we choose the aggressive reply 2.Bf1-c4 is because your opponent might be inspired to respond by bringing his pawn from e7 to e5, leading to precisely the same position you reach in most of your games, which are likely to begin 1.e2-e4 e7-e5; 2.Bf1-c4 Ng8-f6.

2…Nf6xe4. Obviously you must be prepared for Black to capture the pawn, which you have left undefended at e4. On most other moves, you would just bring your knight out from g1 to f3 so that you may castle. If Black tries to switch to the Scandinavian strategy by advancing his pawn to d5, recapture with your pawn, and then bring out your knight and castle as usual.

3.Bc4xf7+. Here's a surprise. You give up your bishop for Black's pawn at f7, bringing the enemy king out into the open. Don't worry, you will soon win the knight at e4 by force, and then the material will be even, despite your sacrificing a pawn and a bishop on consecutive moves.

3...Ke8xf7; 4.Qd1-h5+.

The Black king is in check. If he retreats to g8 or blocks the check by moving the pawn to g6, then you will move your queen to d5, giving check and picking off the knight at e4. After that you can bring out your knight to f3, castle, move the pawn at d4, and bring out the queenside pieces. For example, 4...g7-g6; 5.Qh5-d5+ e7-e6; 6.Qd5xe4. Suppose however, that your opponent is foolish enough to try to save the knight by bringing the king right out into the center of the board?

4...Kf7-f6. The same strategy applies on 4...Kf7-e6. You play 5.Qh5-g4+, and to save the knight, the king must step forward to e5. Then you have the same position you will see below after Black's fifth turn. If the king advances to d5 instead, then you move your pawn from c2 to c4 giving check. If Black captures the pawn, then you capture the knight with check and the Black king is an easy target floating around in the middle of the board.

5.Qh5-f3+ Kf6-e5; 6.d2-d4+.

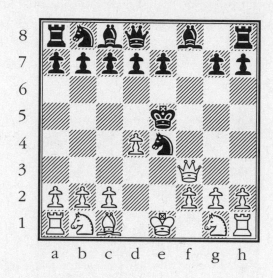

The enemy king is drawn further into your territory. There is no way that he can maintain the position defending his knight for long, and your knights and remaining bishop will quickly drive him away. For example, **6...Ke5xd4; 7.Ng1-e2+ Kd4-e5; 8.Bc1-f4+ Ke5-d5; 9.Nb1-c3+.**

Black cannot capture your knight, because the knight at e4 is pinned to the king by your queen. You will regain your sacrificed piece, and will be able to polish off the enemy king, who is stranded in the middle of the battlefield with absolutely no support.

THE OTHER KNIGHT MOVE

1.e2-e4	Nb8-c6
2.Bf1-c4	

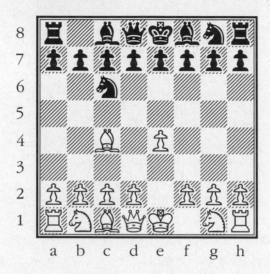

If Black uses his first move to bring the knight out from b8 to c6, then you bring your bishop to c4 and go for the jugular at f7. In this opening, Black does not disclose plans for setting up central pawns. You can't be sure what Black has in mind, so just go about your business.

The guidelines suggest that you advance your pawn from d2 to d4 instead of bringing out the bishop. Objectively, that's the best move. However, Black can then choose from among a wide variety of well-tested strategies, and you would have to prepare for each one. Your attacking move keeps open the possibility of bringing your pawn to d4 at your next turn, unless Black advances the pawn from e7 to e5. In that case, you can be quite happy because you have already prepared this material under the move order 1.e2-e4 e7-e5; 2.Bf1-c4 Nb8-c6.

If Black moves the pawn only one square forward to e6, aiming for a sort of French Defense, then White is assured of a good game since the knight stands badly at c6 in the French. Normally, Black will try to advance the pawn to c5 before bringing out the knight in that opening. Black can also adopt a triangle fianchetto defense by advancing g7 to g6, in which case you set up the formation with a pawn at d4, a pawn at c3, and the queen at e2, as seen in the chapter on the Modern Defense.

2...Ng8-f6. This move attacks your pawn at e4. You cannot safely advance your pawn because Black has a knight at c6, so you must either protect it or be prepared to sacrifice.

3. d2-d4. You are going to offer the pawn at e4 to set up the same trick you use against the Alekhine Defense. You now have two pawns in the center. Black's reasonable choices are limited to either capturing your pawn or advancing the d-pawn to d5 in Scandinavian style.

3...Nxe4. If Black advances the pawn to d5, you capture it and Black takes back with the knight. You are then in a position from the Scandinavian Defense. Black has a knight at c6, so you should support your pawn at d4 by moving its neighbor to c3. Then you can bring out your knight and castle on the kingside as usual.

4.Bxf7+ Kxf7; 5.Qd1-h5+.

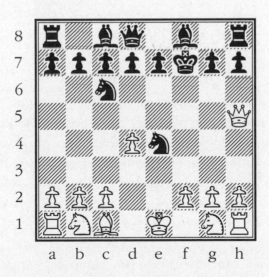

This position is very similar to one that you saw in the chapter on the Alekhine Defense. The only differences are that you have a pawn at d4 and Black has a knight at c6. In this case, the Black king cannot move forward because you control the square e5. So 5...Kf7-e6 can be met by either

6.Qg4-f3+ or 6.d4-d5+, forking the king and knight. Otherwise, the knight is captured with your usual technique.

5…g7-g6; 6.Qh5-d5+ e7-e6 7.Qd5xe4 regains your piece and Black will never be able to castle.

BIZARRE DEFENSES

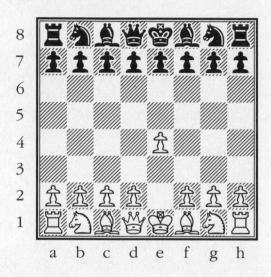

Black has twenty legal moves at the first turn. Each of the pawns can step forward one or two squares, and each of the knights has two possible destinations. Using moves other than those you have examined in previous chapters is quite rare. These moves are considered inferior, and in most cases, all you have to do is follow your basic rules. Move your pawn to d4, bring out the kingside pieces, castle and then work on bringing the rest of your forces into the game. Get your rooks connected and move one of them to the center.

Of course Black can disrupt those plans by employing extreme measures. Sometimes Black will play exclusively on the two flanks and ignore the center entirely. This lets you get your pieces into your preferred fighting formation quickly. Sometimes, however, your pawns or pieces will be confronted by attacks, so you must not mindlessly continue to bring out pieces without examining what your opponent is up to.

YOUR WHITE OPENINGS

You don't really need to be prepared for these openings, except to know a few traps. For example, consider the position after the moves **1.e2-e4 b7-b6; 2.d2-d4 Bc8-b7.**

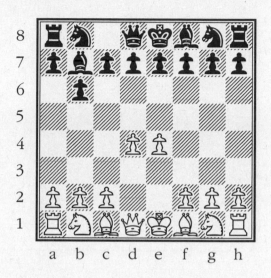

Notice that your pawn at e4 is under attack from the bishop. Before bringing out your kingside pieces, you defend that pawn by moving your knight with **3.Nb1-c3**. This means that you cannot set up your pawn chain from b2 through e5, because the knight will be standing on c3.

However, look at the bishop at b7. Black would surely love for you to move your pawn at e4 so that it can sweep down the entire length of the board. Although you have reliable general guidelines, in chess it is very important to examine each position. Following the formula will not always work. After placing the knight at c3, you can go about your business on the kingside, and get castled. For example, 3...e7-e6; 4.Bf1-d3 Bf8-b4; 5.Ng1-e2.

Let's suppose that Black chooses to play exclusively on the flanks. We'll use as our example an opening known as the **St. George Defense**.

FIRST CHESS OPENINGS

1.e2-e4	a7-a6
2.d2-d4	b7-b5
3.Ng1-f3	Bc8-b7

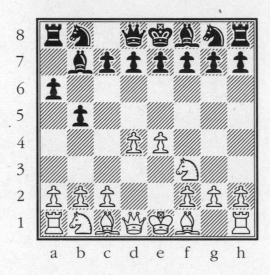

Again your pawn is under attack, but this time, if you bring your knight to c3, the knight can be kicked away when Black's pawn advances to b4. So you defend the pawn with the bishop, playing **4.Bf1-d3**. Now you are prepared to castle at your next turn. There is one ridiculous opening strategy, which is sometimes played as a joke or as a way of giving odds to the opponent.

Black can answer **1.e2-e4** with **1...f7-f5**. In this case, you just capture the pawn and threaten to give check at h5 with a queen.

In order to avoid this grisly fate, Black can respond to **2.e4xf5** with **2...Ng8-f6**. Already you have an extra pawn and Black's kingside is weakened. There is no need to be greedy and hold onto the pawn. Bring your bishop from f1 to d3 to give it some support, then bring out the knight and castle. It's not wise to spend a lot of time preparing for openings that you won't encounter. Once in awhile you may run into something that gives you some trouble. In this case, you can consult some chess literature or online sources and develop a specific strategy for use against any opponent who employs this bizarre plan.

YOUR BLACK OPENINGS

ON BLACK OPENINGS

As Black you will usually be facing the king pawn moved two squares forward. In some cases, you'll have to be prepared to meet the very same openings that you play as White. This cannot be avoided, because your opponent can always choose to play the exact same moves that you like to play. You'll be spending most of your time on these openings, known as the *open games*.

You won't run into other moves as frequently, except the two square advance of the d-pawn, which is popular at all levels of play. Keep things simple and adopt the same formation against all openings other than 1.e2-e4. Establish a strong center with pawns at e6, d5, and c5, put your knights at c6 and f6, bring out your bishop from f8, and castle kingside.

White has the privilege of moving first, and therefore it is easier for White to achieve the four goals of the opening. If White puts a pawn in the center of the board at the first move, it makes it more difficult for you to place both of your pawns in the center. You have to think not only of achieving the four goals, but you must also take advantage of opportunities to prevent White from achieving all four goals. It is highly unlikely that you will successfully place pawns at both d5 and e5 early in the game while still being able to maintain those positions. So as Black, you can be satisfied if you have one pawn in the center. Once that is achieved, you move on to castling and connecting the rooks. Moving a second pawn to the center will usually come only after you have castled, but then it is just unfinished business.

THE MOST COMMON OPENING

1.e2-e4   **e7-e5**

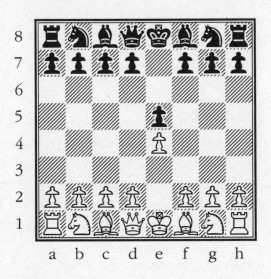

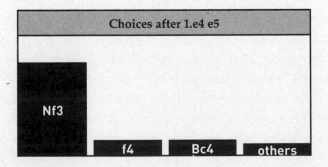

Choices after 1.e4 e5

Nf3

f4

Bc4

others

YOUR BLACK OPENINGS

Most of your games will begin with each player moving their king pawn two squares forward. This prevents either side from establishing the ideal pawn center with two pawns side by side on the fourth rank of the central files. If either side now advances the queen pawn to the center, it can, and almost surely will, be captured.

As White, you would move your bishop to c4, at which point Black can only move the pawn to d5 as a sacrifice. In the remaining chapters of the book we will examine all of the commonly played moves for White at the second turn. If White chooses some other, unusual strategy, just follow the basic plan of bringing your bishop to c5, your knight to f6, and getting castled.

Suppose, for example, White chooses to push a rook pawn forward, say 2.h2-h3. As Black you just play 2…Bf8-c5 and then 3…Ng8-f6, taking aim at White's pawn at e4. It is just as if you were playing White, but here your opponent has an extra move, which has been wasted on advancing the rook pawn.

Some alternatives pose more of a threat. After 2.c2-c3, there is enough support for d4 to chase away your bishop if it moves to c5, so you choose 2…Ng8-f6, attacking the pawn at e4, which cannot be defended by a knight at c3 because there is a pawn sitting on that square. When White plays the pawn to c3, your bishop will usually be best placed at e7.

Let's consider one unprincipled move often seen in games among beginners. With **2.Qd1-h5,** White impudently thrusts the queen into the battlefield, attacking a mere pawn at e5. After you defend the pawn with **2…Nb8-c6**, White can threaten checkmate by playing **3.Bf1-c4**.

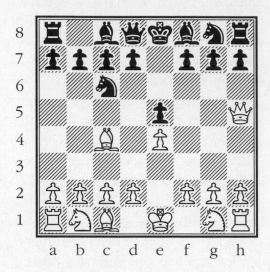

If you aren't careful, Black's next move is Qh5xf7 checkmate. There are several ways to defend against this threat. You could drive back the enemy queen by advancing a pawn to g6. That is a good move, but it is usually followed by putting the bishop at g7, which isn't part of your general plan.

3...Qd8-f6 is a better alternative. On the next turn, bring out bishop to c5. The combined force of the bishop and queen will be brought to bear on f2. Then your knight can move from g8 to e7 and you will be able to castle safely. Keep in mind that with the pawn at e5 guarded by her majesty at f6, your knight at c6 is free to jump to d4 or b4.

Let's get practical now and consider the range of strategies commonly seen after each side has moved the e-pawn to the center. As you see, White chooses 2.Ng1-f3 in most games. That is certainly true for advanced players, but you also might see 2.f2-f4; 2.Nb1-c3; or 2.Bf1-c4 from time to time.

The last choice—the bishop move—is my recommendation for White, though many teachers prefer to plunge right in with the more complicated knight move. We'll examine these moves in detail in later chapters. We have already discussed 2.c2-c3 and 2.Qd1-h5, and most other moves can be handled by your standard plan of bringing the bishop to c5. You can't do that against the gambit move 2.d2-d4, though, because then White could capture your bishop with that pawn. Instead, you'll capture the pawn at d4 with your pawn at e5. We'll get into details later.

Finally, the **Portuguese Opening**—bringing out the bishop to b5 instead of c4—is probably best met by attacking the bishop with a pawn at c6. But meeting 2.Bf1-b5 with 2...Bf8-c5 is also quite good and fits in better with your overall strategy. The impudent White bishop can be evicted later.

After **1.e2-e4 e7-e5; 2.Ng1-f3 Nb8-c6**, White has several important schemes to consider in addition to 3.Bf1-c4, known as the **Italian Game**, which leads to the same position as your main opening for White.

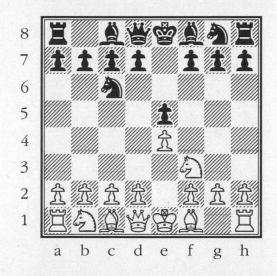

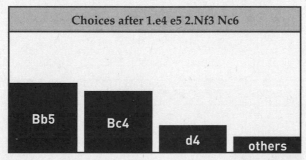

We'll start our coverage with the most popular and complicated line, 3.Bf1-c4, which should be somewhat familiar since you also play it as

White using the move order 2.Bf1-c4 Nb8-c6; 3.Ng1-f3. The move 3.Nb1-c3 can lead in several different directions after 3…Ng8-f6, an opening strategy known as the **Four Knights** that we'll examine later. 3.Bf1-b5 is the famous **Ruy Lopez**, or **Spanish Opening**. If White chooses 3.d2-d4, we'll snatch the pawn.

TWO KNIGHTS ARE GOOD KNIGHTS

1.e2-e4	e7-e5
2.Ng1-f3	Nb8-c6
3.Bf1-c4	Ng8-f6

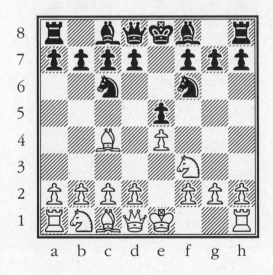

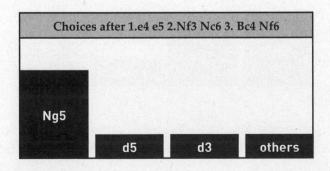

Choices after 1.e4 e5 2.Nf3 Nc6 3. Bc4 Nf6

Ng5   d5   d3   others

This position is the most popular opening in scholastic chess, though it is also seen in top-level professional competition. It is your "magic position" because you face it from both sides of the board. Here as White, you'd move your knight from f3 to g5, but there are other popular moves. 4.Nb1-c3 is covered in the section on the Italian Four Knights. Against 4.c2-c3, just play 4...Nf6xe4, and then 5...d7-d5 on the next move. We'll examine the other three moves, starting with your preferred White move 4.Nf3-g5.

White Tries to Fry Your Liver

1.e2-e4	e7-e5
2.Ng1-f3	Nb8-c6
3.Bf1-c4	Ng8-f6
4.Nf3-g5	d7-d5

You must not allow White to gain access to your weakness at f7. White captures the d-pawn with the pawn from e4, since capturing with the bishop would be a disaster. You could then capture the bishop with your knight, simultaneously unveiling a queen attack against the knight at g5.

5.e4xd5 Nc6-a5.

As you've already seen in the section on the Fried Liver Attack, capturing the pawn at d5 could lead to difficulties. If White sacrifices the knight for your pawn at f7, your king would be brought out into a vulnerable position. By moving your knight to the edge of the board, you attack the bishop at c4 and threaten to capture it on the next turn.

6.Bc4-b5+. If White retreats the bishop to b3, you can capture it with your knight. If the bishop retreats to e2 instead, you just take the pawn at d5 with your knight from f6. This will uncover an attack on White's knight at g5. That leaves moving to b5 with check, which is White's best plan. This is how you should play if you have the White pieces in this position.

6...Bc8-d7. Blocking the check with the pawn is also good, but this plan is simpler.

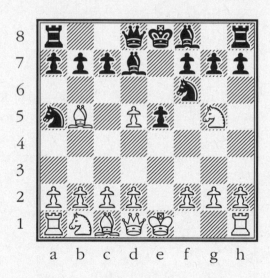

White has eight pawns to Black's seven, and Black's knight at a5 is stranded at the edge of the board. Nevertheless, chances in this position are evaluated as approximately even because Black has more pieces in play and White's pawn at d5 is very weak.

If White exchanges bishops at d7, you recapture with the queen, and will soon pick off the pawn at d5. Among beginners, this is the most common continuation. More advanced players know that the correct move for White is 8.Qd1-e2, defending the bishop while at the same time attacking the Black pawn at e5. You defend against that threat by playing 8...Bf8-d6. Then you are in position to castle, and your king is safe. White's extra pawn at d5 is weak, so you can try to capture it later on in the game.

You can also get rid of it by advancing your own pawn to c6 for an exchange. Don't worry that you are a pawn down. It is not only White who is allowed to play gambit chess. In fact, this variation is considered acceptable even for use in professional competition.

The Quiet Life

1.e2-e4	**e7-e5**
2.Ng1-f3	**Nb8-c6**
3.Bf1-c4	**Ng8-f6**
4.d2-d3	**Bf8-e7**

You are ready to castle and can then move your d-pawn one or two squares so that your bishop can emerge from c8. A sample line is: **6.O-O O-O; 7.Nb1-c3 d7-d6**.

White Offers a Gambit

1.e2-e4	e7-e5
2.Ng1-f3	Nb8-c6
3.Bf1-c4	Ng8-f6
4.d2-d4	e5xd4

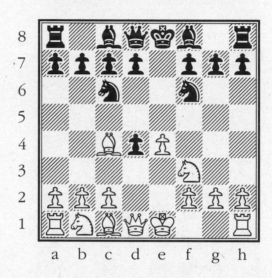

Advancing the pawn to d4 and allowing you to capture it, is a very aggressive plan for White. The pawn at d4 can be recaptured right away, but there are three alternative plans that also deserve consideration. We'll focus on the most complicated and dangerous line: **5.e4-e5.**

If White simply castles, you could capture the pawn at e4, which is not defended. However, that opens up a line against your king, with no pawn barriers standing on the e-file. Instead, let's decline the offer and bring your bishop from f8 to c5. That way your pawn at d4 has extra support and you are ready to castle.

White can also try the plan of attack against f7 by moving the knight to g5, but after 5.Nf3-g5 you play 5…Nc6-e5, attacking White's bishop and defending f7 at the same time. If the bishop stays in place, you capture it at the next turn. If the bishop retreats, you advance your h-pawn to h6, driving away the enemy knight.

Should White choose to play 5.Nf3xd4, recovering the pawn immediately, you again play 5...Bf8-c5. The knight is then attacked twice, and you are ready to castle. If White then plays 6.Nd4xc6, you recapture 6...b7xc6, following the general rule that you should choose to capture toward the center of the board whenever possible.

This also avoids the exchange of queens that would be available if you used your d-pawn. White can advance the pawn to attack your knight, but then the knight jumps to e4, and you have a double attack against f2. Things can get a little hairy after the sacrifice 7.Bc4xf7+ Ke8xf7; 8.Qd1-f3+, but if this happens just retreat the knight with 8...Ne4-f6. If your opponent captures the knight with the pawn, don't immediately recapture with the queen. Instead, toss a check by moving your rook to e8. After White deals with the check you can capture the pawn at f6 with your queen.

Advancing the pawn to attack your knight is the most ambitious plan. Since the pawn is guarded by the knight at f3, you seem to have little choice but to move your knight from f6. In fact, you can launch a surprising counterattack by moving your pawn to d5 to attack White's bishop.

5...Nf6-e4!

In general, when White advances the pawn from e4 to e5, your knight can take up a position at e4. It looks a little risky, standing alone in the middle of the board, but the knight does have an escape route via c5. Whenever you place a piece in an exposed position, you need to ensure that it can escape if necessary. For example 6.Bc4-d5 Ne4-c5.

6.O-O. Castling is the most logical move, though you'll often see White playing the queen out to attack your knight. On 6.Qd1-e2, simply retreat your knight to c5, and it can then move to e6.

When the knight reaches e6, it will not only provide additional protection for the pawn at f7 by blocking the diagonal a2-g8, but it will also defend your extra pawn at d4. Your pawn at d4 can receive extra support from a bishop at c5. In any case, you will quickly bring that bishop into the game and get castled yourself. Sometimes White is foolish enough to capture the pawn at d4 with the knight, but this leaves the White pawn at e5 undefended and you can collect that with your knight at c6.

DEFINITION

In case you aren't aware of the **en passant** rule, it allows the capture of a pawn which advances two squares so that the pawn moves to a position next to an enemy pawn along a rank. The idea is that though the pawn goes two squares, it can't escape capture just by doing so. The pawn is captured just as if it had advanced one square. The rules were modified hundreds of years ago to speed up the game, but it was decided that the two-square move could not be used to slip past an enemy pawn that might capture it.

Finally, White can offer a gambit by moving the pawn at c2 to c3. Instead of capturing that pawn, I recommend that you move your pawn from d7 to d5, just as you will below when White has castled. Then the bishop at c4 is under attack. White can capture the pawn using the *en passant* rule.

On 6.c2-c3 d7-d5; 7.e5xd6, you capture the pawn at d6 with your knight from e4. Again, White's bishop at c4 is under attack, and there is an additional benefit because the knight defends the pawn at f7.

6...d7-d5.

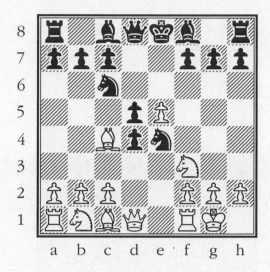

The bishop at c4 is under attack and White must either retreat it, advance to b5, or capture the pawn at d5 by using the en passant rule. If White does play 7.e5xd6, you recapture with the knight, attacking the bishop at c4. The next move will get your bishop from f8 to e7 and then you will be able to castle. So, more frequently White moves the bishop to d5 to pin your knight at c6 and make the recovery of the pawn at d4 a bit simpler.

7.Bc4-b5 Bc8-d7. The pin is broken and you will be able to develop your bishop from f8 and castle in the next few moves. White can regain the gambit pawn but that is of no real concern to you.

You should keep in mind that one of the best ways to deal with a gambit by your opponent is to capture the gambit pawn but not try to hold onto it. Let your opponent waste time recovering the pawn while you attend to more serious matters. This not only gives you a more secure position, but can also be very frustrating to the player who enjoys sacrificing a pawn and watching a greedy opponent get tangled up trying to defend it.

White Castles

1.e2-e4	e7-e5
2.Ng1-f3	Nb8-c6
3.Bf1-c4	Ng8-f6
4.O-O	

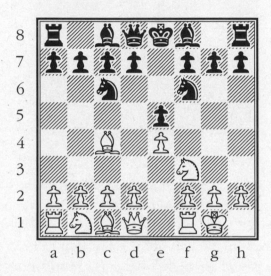

You may be surprised to learn that this move is seen almost exclusively in amateur-level games, primarily because it leaves the pawn at e4 undefended. Indeed, the game can proceed into the territory of the Boden Gambit, which you play as White. However, because White has already castled you can play the gambit in a way that avoids all of the problems for Black.

4...Nf6xe4; 5.Nb1-c3. This is the gambit line. Many beginners will attempt to recover the pawn right away, and you should be prepared to meet these moves although they cause no particular difficulties. The most obvious move is 5.Rf1-e1, attacking your knight. This is easily handled by 5...d7-d5, when your pawn both defends your knight at e4 and attacks the White's bishop at c4. Generally, when White does not play the knight out to c3 at the fifth turn, moving the d-pawn to d5 is the correct response.

5...Ne4xc3; 6.d2xc3 Bf8-e7.

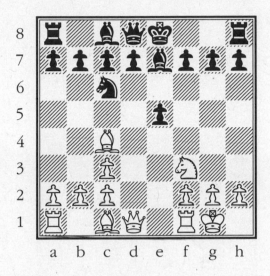

As you can see, Black is ready to castle, after which the d-pawn can be advanced and the bishop can emerge from c8. White can recover the sacrificed pawn by playing 7.Qd1-d5, threatening checkmate at f7. After 7...O-O; 8.Nf3xe5 Nc6xe5; 9.Qd5xe5, you slide your bishop to f6, attacking the enemy queen. You then have a superior position because your pawn structure is better and you have the initiative because White must deal with the attack on the queen. This concludes our examination of the Italian game.

Quite a lot of material was presented, but the Italian is the most common opening you will face. If you remember to castle early in the game you will not face any particular problems in this opening. Now we move on to the infamous Spanish Inquisition.

DON'T BE AFRAID OF THE SPANISH INQUISITION

1.e2-e4	e7-e5
2.Ng1-f3	Nb8-c6
3.Bf1-b5	

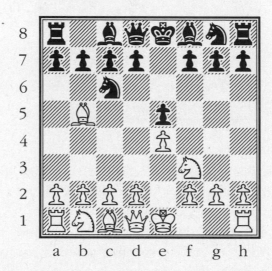

The **Spanish Game**, also known as the **Ruy Lopez**, is one of the oldest openings and one of the most common in both amateur and professional play. There is actually a lot less immediate danger for Black in these lines because the bishop does not point at the vulnerable f7 square. There are no early attacks against the king. Black will have no difficulty bringing out pieces and getting castled, but White will hold onto a bit more of the center and usually enjoys a small initiative.

3...Ng8-e7

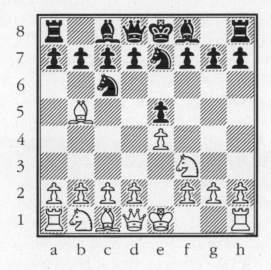

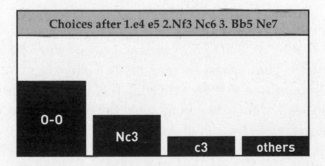

White was threatening to capture a knight at c6, leaving the pawn at e5 defenseless. Advanced and professional players do not fear this threat, because although the queenside pawns will be messed up when Black recaptures, Black will then enjoy an advantage of having a pair of bishops.

Normally, having two bishops and one knight is better than having two knights and one bishop. The bishops are affective long range pieces. However, playing with a shattered pawn structure is not easy for beginners. The pawn's permanent weakness, often leads to trouble late in the game. To combat this, I recommend the **Cozio Defense.** Even though it is somewhat rare for beginners, it is a good enough opening to be seen even in professional competition.

At higher levels it is considered less promising than the major variations. Playing the major lines require quite a bit of preparation. Beginners don't need to spend huge amounts of time learning the opening. The Cozio approach is very easy to learn, and can be very frustrating to White.

The main point is that if White captures the knight at c6 with the bishop, Black will be able to recapture with the knight. In that case, White will have exchanged a valuable bishop for a slightly less valuable knight without receiving the benefit of shattering the queenside pawn structure.

There is an important subtle point as well. Normally, when White captures the knight and forces a pawn recapture, Black is more or less required to retake with the pawn at d7, not the one at b7. This captures away from the center, which—except in the case of gambits—is not advisable.

To understand this point, play through the following moves: 1.e2-e4 e7-e5; 2.Ng1-f3 Nb8-c6; 3.Bf1-b5 a7-a6; 4.Bb5xc6 d7xc6; 5.Nf3xe5 Qd8-d4. The queen attacks both the knight and White's pawn at e4, so at the very least the sacrificed pawn will be recovered. If Black had captured with the pawn at b7 instead of the pawn at d7, then the queen would be unable to carry out this maneuver.

Your strategy will be to attack the bishop at b5 with a pawn on the next turn. If the bishop captures the knight, then you will recapture with your knight from e7. If the bishop retreats to a4, you will be able to attack it again with a pawn at b5.

After these preliminaries you will transfer your knight from e7—if it is still there—to g6. Then you can bring out the bishop and castle. Because White chose to aim the bishop at your knight at c6 rather than your weak pawn at f7, you are under no pressure to defend that square and can adopt this more patient strategy. One of the main reasons I have recommended this strategy for Black is that White usually responds with very predictable moves. You can see this in the graph on the previous page.

On 4.Nb1-c3 or 4.d2-d3, you should go after the bishop with …a7-a6 and b7-b5. The game is not substantially different from the play after White castles at the fourth turn. The only distinct variations you need to learn are 4.O-O and 4.c2-c3, which prepares an early advance of the queen pawn, as well as the immediate 4.d2-d4. We'll examine these options next.

White Castles

1.e2-e4	e7-e5
2.Ng1-f3	Nb8-c6
3.Bf1-b5	Ng8-e7
4.O-O	a7-a6
5.Bb5-a4	

You aren't the least bit afraid of White capturing your knight, because you are ready to recapture with your other knight. Then the bishop comes out and you castle.

5...b7-b5.

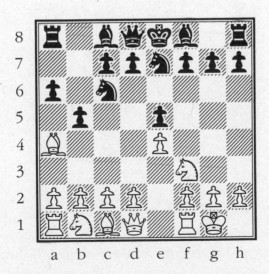

When the bishop retreats to b3, you have the initiative. Both sides have one pawn in the center and have two pieces in the game. However since

White has already castled, you have to play catch-up. You are going to move your knight to g6, bring out your bishop, and get castled. The only important decision you will have in the next few moves is how to deal with White moving the pawn from d2 to d4.

6.Ba4-b3 Ne7-g6; 7.d2-d4. This is the one move you have to prepare for. It causes a little discomfort because you may have to postpone castling for a bit. On 7.c2-c3 Bf8-e7 you are ready to castle. If White chooses 8.d2-d4, you castle anyway. Should White's pawn advance to d5, your knight can go to a5, attacking the bishop, and then to c4 if the bishop retreats.

If White chooses to push the d-pawn to the center without a preliminary advance of the c-pawn, you capture the pawn with **7...e5xd4.** Don't use the knight, because then White's knight will cause problems at g5, attacking f7. After **8.Nf3xd4 Nc6xd4; 9.Qd1xd4 Bc8-b7** we reach the following position.

The move of the bishop prevents White from playing the queen to d5, where she would threaten checkmate at f7 as well as the unprotected rook at a8. It is important to understand the strategy of this position. Even though White's queen is exposed in the center of the board, you don't want to go after her with moves like c7-c5. That would weaken your pawn structure, because the pawn at d7 would be stranded as a backward pawn.

The easiest way to play this position is to move your queen to e7 and then to c5 or e5, offering an exchange of queens. You also have a threat of advancing your pawn to c5 attacking the queen, and then pushing it one square further, trapping White's bishop.

There is a little trick here that you should be aware of, even though it is extremely unlikely that your opponent would spot it. White can play **10.Rf1-d1**. Then if Black plays 10...c7-c5, White has the surprising resource 11.Bb3xf7+ Ke8xf7; 12.Qd4xd7+ Qd8-e7 (otherwise White grabs the bishop at b7); 13.Bc1-g5, after which your bishop at b7 is doomed. Instead, just answer the rook move with **10...Qd8-e7!**, renewing the threat. Your queen can later go to e5 or c5, giving you time to get the bishop out and castle.

Even though I haven't seen this line of play in competition, it seems reasonable that you might run into it. Since it doesn't follow the usual guideline of castling quickly, it is important to be familiar with it.

White Builds a Big Center

1.e2-e4	e7-e5
2.Ng1-f3	Nb8-c6
3.Bf1-b5	Ng8-e7
4.c2-c3	a7-a6

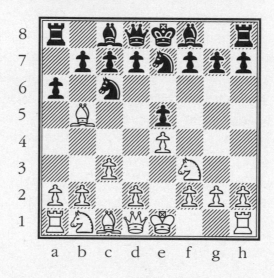

Advancing the pawn to c3 is an excellent way to prepare the central advance of the queen pawn. However, since it doesn't pose any immediate threat, you have time to annoy White's bishop. When you attack the bishop with the pawn, the bishop should retreat, since capturing your knight falls in with your plans and you recapture with the knight.

5.Bb5-a4 b7-b5; 6.Ba4-c2. If the bishop retreats to b3 instead, then you move your knight to g6. Play will then be similar to that of the previous section, especially if White castles as expected.

6...Ne7-g6; 7.d2-d4. Castling leads to the same sort of positions as you've seen above, except that the bishop at c2 is not particularly helpful when the pawn at e4 stands in the way.

The pawn at d4 attacks the pawn at e5 and also threatens to step forward and drive your knight away. In the previous section, White's bishop stood at b3 rather than at c2 so that when you moved the knight to the edge of the board at a5, you would at least threaten the bishop. That's not the case here.

7...e5xd4. I recommend that you capture the pawn. If White recaptures with the pawn from c3, you can move your bishop into checking position at b4 and then castle. If White plays 8.Nf3xd4, play 8...Bc8-b7 to give extra support to your knight at c6. Then bring out the other bishop and castle.

The Immediate Break in the Center

1.e2-e4	e7-e5
2.Ng1-f3	Nb8-c6
3.Bf1-b5	Ng8-e7
4.d2-d4	

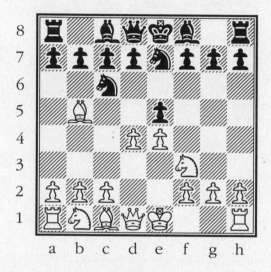

This is a very provocative move. White's pawn can capture the pawn at e5 or can step forward and go after the knight at c6.

4...e5xd4; 5.Nf3xd4 Nc6xd4; 6.Qd1xd4 Nd7-c6. If White captures the knight you use the b-pawn to recapture. Otherwise the queen must retreat.

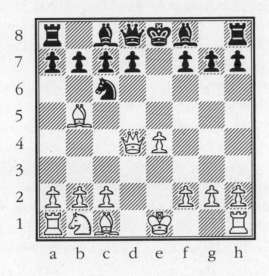

7.Bb5xc6. If the queen moves you can play your queen to e7, then move it to e5, c5, or b4. For example, on 7.Qd4-d5 Qd8-e7; 8.Bb5-c4, aiming for tricks at f7, White runs into serious trouble after 8…Nc6-b4.

7…b7xc6; 8.O-O d7-d6!

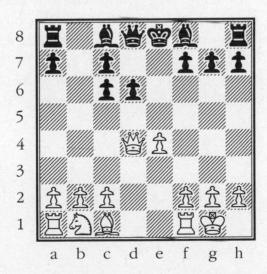

If White is clever enough to castle after capturing the knight, you have to be a little bit careful. If White manages to open up the e-file and you have not castled, the rook will have a devastating effect at e1. However, your move is equally clever. If White advances the pawn to e5, you will sidestep the pawn by moving your pawn to d5. Then the e-file remains closed and you can bring out your bishop and castle.

Instead of pushing the pawn right away, White can bring the rook to d1, but that makes no difference since again, in reply to a future step forward by the pawn, Black can sidestep by advancing the pawn at d6 to d5.

You might be wondering how you are going to be able to castle here without losing your pawn at g7. That is actually a very simple matter. White only puts pressure on your pawn at g7 if the queen stays at d4. You can use a timely advance of your c-pawn to kick her out. For example, if White brings out the knight from b1 to c3 now, you play your pawn to c5 and the queen cannot retreat to c3 because the knight is sitting on that square.

Suppose you get to this position and White plays 9.Rf1-e1. You answer 9…c6-c5; 10.Qd4-c3 Bc8-e6 followed by f7-f6, Bf8-e7 and castling. Your king is never in any danger. Eventually, your bishop at e7 will come alive after either the f-pawn or d-pawn gets out of the way.

In this variation, you accept some weaknesses in your pawn structure, but it is in return for the bishop pair. However, this position does not resemble the dreaded exchange variation, since Black has managed to capture at c6 with the pawn from b7, not d7. In this position, Black can look forward to advancing the pawn from c6 to c5 and then station a bishop at b7. Alternatively, the bishop can come from c8 to e6 and aim at the queenside.

WHITE OPENS UP THE CENTER

Instead of bringing out a bishop at the third turn, White can advance the d-pawn to d4, with several options of playing it as a gambit.

1.e2-e4	e7-e5
2.Ng1-f3	Nb8-c6
3.d2-d4	e5xd4

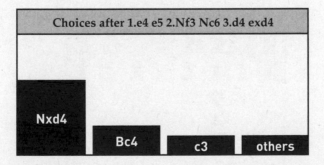

Choices after 1.e4 e5 2.Nf3 Nc6 3.d4 exd4

Nxd4 Bc4 c3 others

White can of course capture the pawn at d4 and keep the level of force equal. However, a variety of gambits have been explored and some are very popular. You need to be prepared for three different gambit moves as well as the recapture of the pawn. As you can see, capturing the pawn at d4 is White's most popular option by far. The second most popular move, bringing the bishop to c4, reaches a position we have already discussed in the Two Knights Defense in the section "White Offers a Gambit."

White reaches the position by different move orders, but whether the bishop goes to c4 first or the pawn is put at d4 first doesn't matter. So if White brings the bishop to c4, you bring your knight out from g8 to f6 reaching the Two Knights Opening already discussed.

The remaining gambit approaches are rare and not difficult to counter. If White advances a pawn to c3, Black will counter in the center by moving the pawn from d7 to d5. You have already seen this typical counter blow used on a number of occasions. Finally, moving the bishop to b5 is a very rare gambit, though it is one I have used myself on a number of occasions. Here, too, you will return the gambit pawn and continue your path toward castling by bringing out your knight to f6.

Normal Play in the Center

1.e2-e4	e7-e5
2.Ng1-f3	Nb8-c6
3.d2-d4	e5xd4
4.Nf3xd4	Bf8-c5

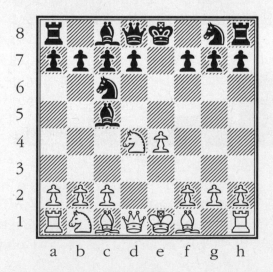

YOUR BLACK OPENINGS

By attacking the knight at d4, you briefly seize the initiative. White has to do something about the problem at d4. White can exchange knights, retreat the knight, or defend the knight. The exchange of knights is the variation we will concentrate on, as the others are fairly easy to deal with.

If White retreats the knight to b3, attacking the bishop, move your bishop to b6. White might then push the pawn from a2 to a4, threatening to go to a5 and trapping your bishop. So, in response to a2-a4, move your a-pawn two squares forward to a5. If the knight retreats to f3 instead, move your pawn from d7 to d6, and then bring your knight out to f6 and castle.

The best way to protect the knight at d4 is to bring out the bishop. If White uses the c-pawn instead, then just bring your knight out to f6. But after 5.Bc1-e3, things get a lot more interesting. White threatens to capture your knight at c6, and then grab the bishop at c5 with the bishop from e3. Most advanced players like to meet this threat by bringing the queen out to f6.

That's quite a complicated variation, so let's settle for the simple move 5...Bc5-b6. Now your bishop is perfectly safe and there are no tricks that can embarrass you. On the next turn you can bring your knight to either f6 or e7 and then castle. This is a simple and solid way to play for Black.

Now that we've covered the other lines, let's move on to the exchange of knights at c6. When White captures, you will have a surprise in store.

5.Nd4xc6 Qd8-f6!

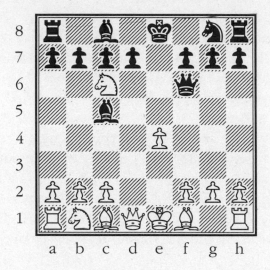

If you are really lucky, your opponent will overlook the fact that you're threatening checkmate by capturing the pawn at f2 with your queen. Even if White notices the threat, defending against it is rather awkward. If White brings the queen to f3, you can either capture the queen in a trade, or use your queen to capture White's knight. This little tactical checkmate trick allows you to capture that knight without messing up your pawn structure. By the way, you have another little trick in store if you follow these moves: 6.Qd1-f3 Qf6xc6; 7.Bf1-c4 Bc5xf2+! After White captures your bishop you can take the bishop at c4 with your queen.

6.Qd1-d2. This ugly move, smothering the bishop at c1, is not only considered best, but it is also far and away the most common move in that situation.

6...Qf6xc6. Advanced players prefer capturing with the pawn at d7, but because that move runs counter to some of your general principles, and creates a weakness in the pawn structure, it will be easier if you capture with the queen. Then you can bring out the knight, castle and move the pawn from b7 so that your bishop can emerge from c8. The rest of the opening should proceed smoothly.

White Gambit with C-Pawn

1.e2-e4	e7-e5
2.Ng1-f3	Nb8-c6
3.d2-d4	e5xd4
4.c2-c3	d7-d5

This gambit is known to be quite tricky if the pawn at c3 is captured, but by moving the pawn from d7 to d5, Black totally refutes White's opening strategy. Ask most gambit fans why they don't play this particular gambit, and they might just look at you and say, "d5."

Because you attack the pawn at e4, White usually captures the pawn at d5. This will lead to a position where, in the end, White will have a weak isolated pawn at d4. The following moves are common: **5.e4xd5 Qd8xd5; 6.c3xd4 Bc8-g4; 7.Bf1-e2 Bf8-b4+**. Black has a comfortable position, and indeed can lay claim to the initiative.

Gambit in Spanish Style

1.e2-e4	e7-e5
2.Ng1-f3	Nb8-c6
3.d2-d4	e5xd4
4.Bf1-b5	Ng8-f6

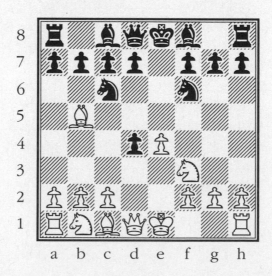

YOUR BLACK OPENINGS

You don't need a lot of preparation to play this position. By allowing White to recapture the pawn, the game transfers to the territory of the Spanish game, into a well-known harmless variation. White can follow many different paths, but in each case all you have to do is bring out your bishop and then castle. The only tactical consideration is the possibility of White's pawn advancing to e5, and attacking your knight. Keep in mind that if White captures your knight with his bishop, you should recapture towards the center by using the pawn at b7.

White captures your knight at c6 and you recapture with the pawn from b7. If White captures the pawn at d4 with the knight, you exchange knights. After 5.Nf3xd4 Nc6xd4; 6.Qd1xd4, you play 7...a7-a6, and play is similar to that of the Cozio Defense you play as Black in the Spanish Game, except that your knight is at f6. On 8.Bb5-a4, you can play 8...c7-c5, threatening to suffocate the bishop at b3, by playing b7-b5 and then c5-c4. White then has to move the attacked queen to e5, giving check. In this case you can block the check with the bishop and then castle.

5.e4-e5 Nf6-e4! Remember, when White advances a pawn to e5 in an open game where your pawn has disappeared, the knight should usually go to e4. You just have to be careful to make sure that the knight can either escape to c5 or g5, or be defended by advancing a pawn to d5 or f5.

This means that you probably don't want to put your bishop at c5. Place the bishop in a more modest position at e7 and then castle. For example: **6.O-O Bf8-e7; 7.Rf1-e1 Ne4-c5; 8.Nf3xd4 Nc6xd4; 9.Qd1xd4 O-O.**

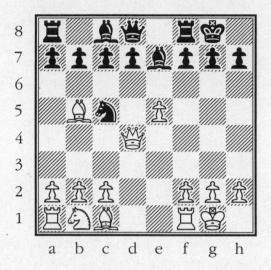

You can be very happy with this position. Your bishop at c8 will most likely enter the game at b7 after the pawn advances. You can move the pawn from d7 to d6 to challenge White's pawn at e5. If necessary, your knight can retreat to e6 and attack White's queen.

ALL FOUR KNIGHTS

1.e2-e4	**e7-e5**
2.Ng1-f3	**Nb8-c6**
3.Nb1-c3	**Ng8-f6**

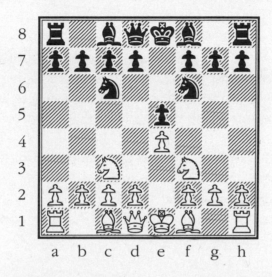

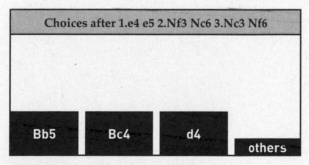

Bringing out all four knights early in the game is seen very frequently in games played by beginners and amateurs, but is much more rare among more experienced players. That's because it isn't very interesting. Put plainly, it can lead to extremely boring positions.

There are a few ways to spice it up, but after awhile most players tire of the approach as White. There are several different strategies White can pursue at this point. The bishop can be used in Spanish style at b5 or in the Italian style at c4.

White can also open up the center by moving the pawn to d4, known as the Scotch approach since it is very similar to the Scotch game we looked at earlier. A recent book advocated moving the pawn from a2-a3 in this position, throwing the burden of selecting a strategy on Black's shoulders, although Black could choose to continue the symmetry by moving his own a-pawn.

We'll be looking at the international smorgasbord of approaches in detail, but as far as the last proposal is concerned let's dismiss it quickly. On 4.a2-a3, just move your bishop to e7 and then castle. The leading proponent of this approach for White admits that this is probably the best way to defend.

White can also adopt a fianchetto plan, putting a bishop at g2 after moving the pawn to g3. This can be handled the same way. Let's now consider the Italian, Spanish, and Scotch methods of playing the Four Knights. These are the main lines, or the plans your opponent is most likely to use.

Four Knights, Italian Style

1.e2-e4	e7-e5
2.Ng1-f3	Nb8-c6
3.Nb1-c3	Ng8-f6
4.Bf1-c4	Bf8-e7

It is important to bring the bishop into the game and castle. You don't want White to bring the knight to g5 unless you can castle. You usually put the bishop at e7, because as Black you must concentrate on fending off White's attack in the opening. Fortunately, you are about to castle and then you can turn your attention to more ambitious plans.

5.O-O O-O; 6.d2-d3 d7-d6. As the game progresses, you will try to bring your bishop from c8 to g4. There is one advantage of having your bishop at e7. If White moves a bishop to g5, your knight at f6 is not pinned, because the bishop stands between the knight and the queen.

If your bishop does get to g4, the pin on the knight can become painful, especially if you pile on the pressure by bringing your knight from c6 to d4.

Four Knights, Spanish Style

1.e2-e4	e7-e5
2.Ng1-f3	Nb8-c6
3.Nb1-c3	Ng8-f6
4.Bf1-b5	d7-d6

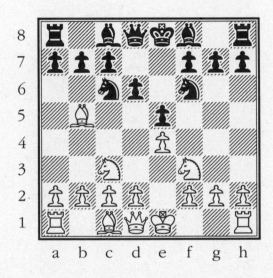

Against the Spanish Four Knights, you are going to switch your move order around a bit. Your bishop will eventually wind up at e7. At the moment, you do have to take care of your pawn at e5 because White might capture the knight at c6 and remove the defender of the pawn. White has a knight at c3, so it won't be easy for you to win White's pawn at e4 if you give up your pawn at e5.

First you have to protect the pawn, then you bring out the bishop and castle, keeping in mind the possibility of bringing your bishop from c8 to g4 earlier if you wish. The only popular move for White now is to try to smash open the center, as quieter plans allow you to peacefully carry out your remaining opening tasks.

5.d2-d4 e5xd4; 6.Nf3xd4. There are no useful gambits for White because the knight at c3 was under attack, so the pawn had to be recaptured. White could capture the pawn with the queen, since your knight at c6 is pinned to the king by the bishop at b5. However, it is a trivial matter to break the pin by moving a bishop to d7 so the queen would find herself embarrassed and exposed in the middle of the board.

6...Bc8-d7. The pin is broken and Black can continue with the usual plan of placing the bishop at e7 and castle.

Four Knights, Scotch Style

1.e2-e4	e7-e5
2.Ng1-f3	Nb8-c6
3.Nb1-c3	Ng8-f6
4.d2-d4	e5xd4

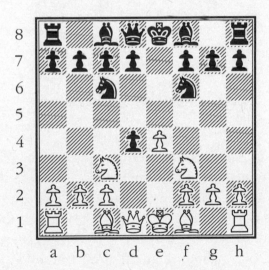

5.Nf3xd4. White does not have to capture this pawn. There is a well-established gambit approach, moving the knight to d5. It isn't the sort of gambit you are likely to encounter as a beginner.

Still, here's how I suggest you handle it when you do encounter it: 5.Nc3-d5 Bf8-e7. As usual you put a bishop at e7. White can capture it with the knight, but then you recapture with the queen and, for the moment, you have an extra pawn as well as pressure against White's pawn at e4.

Although bishops are considered marginally more valuable than knights, it really all depends on what sort of view the bishop has. In your defensive scheme, you often put a pawn at d6, leaving the bishop at e7 to attend to purely defensive duties. In this case, it isn't bad for you when White exchanges a knight, standing proudly in the center of the board, for your modest cleric.

5...Bf8-b4!

You will want to remember this move, because you are sending your bishop out on a serious errand for a change. Your bishop pins White's knight at c3, leaving the pawn at e4 with no available defender. You threaten to capture it with your knight, putting White on the defensive.

At the same time, you are now ready to castle. In general, your bishop has a less glorious duty, standing guard at e7. But when your opponent gives you a chance to put the bishop to better use, you should take advantage of the challenge.

White has to deal with the immediate threat, and usually plays **6.Nd4xc6 b7xc6; 7.Bf1-d3 O-O; 8.O-O.** Then you can confront White's center by moving the pawn from d7 to d5.

YOUR BLACK OPENINGS

WHITE USES YOUR OWN OPENING AGAINST YOU

1.e2-e4	e7-e5
2.Bf1-c4	Ng8-f6

You'll recognize this position, because as White you will see it in most of your games. Here you are concerned with how to defend it as Black. Although we prefer to play 3.Ng1-f3, you can see from the chart that most players prefer moving the pawn to d3, keeping open the option of playing the pawn from f2 to f4 before bringing the knight to f3.

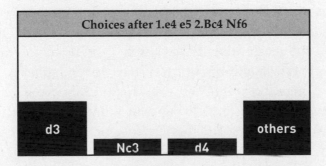

Choices after 1.e4 e5 2.Bc4 Nf6

Before moving on to the main line, lets deal with the other moves. If White plays 3.d2-d4, you capture 3...e5xd4. Then White almost always brings out the knight to f3, reaching the position we have already discussed in the Scotch Gambit. If White pushes the pawn to e5 instead, you use a familiar strategy and ignore the pawn, choosing to attack White's bishop at c4 by bringing your pawn out. After 4.e4-e5 d7-d5! White can capture the d-pawn at d6 by using the en passant rule, but is more likely to give check with the bishop at b5. That position is worth looking at.

You have to be a little bit careful here because your knight at f6 is under attack. You might think that the best way to deal with this position would be to retreat the knight from f6 to d7, or to block at c6 with the pawn so that if White captures your knight you could capture the bishop.

However, there is a much more effective move. You can block the check with your bishop. If White then captures your knight at f6, you use your bishop to capture White's bishop at b5. If White captures your bishop at d7, giving check, you recapture with the knight from f6, removing it from the danger zone. This is an important trick, so try to remember it.

If White brings the knight out from b1 to c3, or from g1 to f3, don't move the pawn to d4. Instead, bring your knight from b8 to c6, heading for a variation of the Two Knights Defense or the Italian Four Knights.

Sometimes White will play 3.Nb1-c3 Nb8-c6 4.f2-f4, but this is a mistake because you have a tactical refutation. You can capture White's e-pawn with 4...Nf6xe4!, because after White captures your knight with 5.Nc3xe4, you can fork the knight and bishop by playing 5...d7-d5.

Of course if White brings the knight out from g1 to f3 at the third turn, you reach the Two Knights Defense when you bring your knight from b8 to c6, reaching the Gambit Variation we have already looked at. So, that just leaves the most popular move, advancing the d-pawn one square.

3.d2-d3 Nb8-c6.

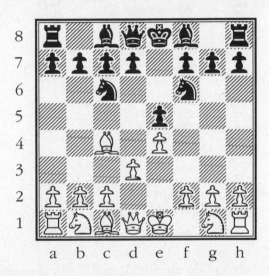

If White brings out one of the knights, the game will head toward the territory of the Two Knights or Four Knights. The only strategy to give the game a somewhat different flavor is when White advances the pawn to f4, either immediately or after bringing a knight to c3.

4.f2-f4. 4.Nb1-c3 is best handled by bringing your bishop to b4, pinning the knight to the king. Normally you would place your bishop at e7 and castle. However, an early advance of the d-pawn combined with a knight at c3 makes the alternative at b4 attractive.

You can also just play the bishop to e7, to reach more familiar positions. The strategies are equally effective, and in both cases you can already be satisfied with the results of the opening.

4...Bf8-c5. Again, there is nothing wrong with simply moving your bishop to e7. However, the advance of the f-pawn seriously weakens White's king position. By placing your bishop at c5, you make it very difficult for White to castle.

5.Ng1-f3 d7-d6. Castling is an immediate option, but by advancing your d-pawn, you make it possible for the bishop to come from c8 to g4. The pin on the knight at f3 will be very annoying for White.

This position is easy to play for Black. You'll pin the knight at f3 unless White stops you. Castle kingside and then move the queen up so that your rooks are connected. Your opponent, unable to castle, will have a much more difficult time meeting the requirements of the four goals discussed in the early chapters of the book.

THE FAMOUS KING'S GAMBIT

1.e2-e4	e7-e5
2.f2-f4	d7-d5

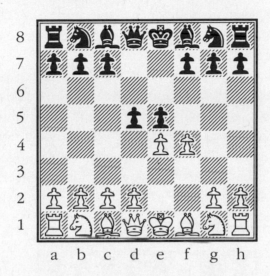

Usually, you react to a gambit by capturing the offered pawn and then letting the opponent spend a lot of time getting it back. In the **King's Gambit**, you could capture the pawn at f4 right away, but in that case you would have to learn a variety of strategies to combat White's many options. Instead, you are going to use a little finesse. You will indeed capture the pawn at f4, but first you plant a second pawn in the center by bringing your d-pawn to d5.

Already, White faces a serious decision. Normally, White will capture your pawn at d5. Capturing the pawn at e5 instead would be a tremendous blunder, because you would achieve an almost winning position by bringing your queen out from d8 to h4 giving check against the enemy king while at the same time threatening the pawn at e4. So White's playable options are limited to capturing the pawn at d5 or defending the pawn at e4.

3.e4xd5. Should White choose to defend the pawn at e4, just capture it, bring out your pieces and castle. This isn't likely to happen, as White captures at d5 in over 95 percent of all games featuring this position.

3...e5xf4! This sensible move may come as a little bit of a surprise to your opponent. When Black advances the pawn to d5 on the second turn, the intention is usually to play the opening as a gambit.

Instead of capturing at f4, Black can choose between advancing the pawn from e5 to e4, or offering an exchange by pushing the pawn from c7 to c6. Both of these are more popular than the capture at f4, but that's only because Black normally captures at f4 on the second move if the intention is to accept the King's Gambit.

4.Ng1-f3. White usually plays this move, since normally when the King's Gambit is accepted the knight quickly takes up a position at f3.

Most importantly, the knight at f3 prevents Black from bringing the queen to h4 and giving check. As Black, you should throw the check if White allows you to do so. The only other reasonable move to prevent the check is to bring the bishop to b5, giving check to the Black king. You can block with the bishop, or with the pawn. Both are good moves.

4...Bc8-g4.

Black has many options. The pawn at d5 can be captured by the queen, the knight can come out to f6 to grab the pawn later, the bishop can move from f8 to d6 to defend the pawn at f4, etc. I recommend that you pin the knight and don't be in too much of a hurry to grab the pawn at d5. When you capture the pawn with your queen, White gains time by bringing the knight out from b1 to c3, placing her under attack. White will most likely move the bishop from f1 now. Either it will go to e2, to break the pin, or to b5, giving check.

5.Bf1-b5+ c7-c6; 6.d5xc6 and now you can either recapture the pawn at c6, or try a more interesting plan. **6...Qd8-e7+** puts White in an awkward position. The king does not want to move, because that would give up the right to castle. If the bishop retreats from b5 to e2, you can comfortably recapture at c6 with the knight.

Most likely, White will block the check with the queen, allowing you to exchange queens. Then you can recapture the pawn at c6. The pawn structure will be unbalanced, with White having the advantage on the queenside, and Black having a large advantage on the kingside. Chances are about equal.

WHITE BRINGS OUT THE OTHER KNIGHT

1.e2-e4	e7-e5
2.Nb1-c3	Nb8-c6

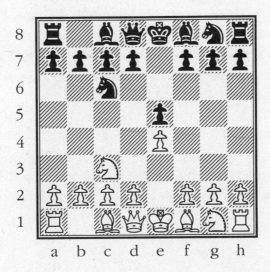

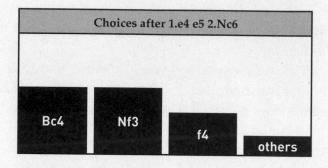

This opening, called the **Vienna Game**, is rare. The knight at c3 doesn't threaten anything, and the game is likely to lead into one of the paths we have already explored. Still, Black has to be a little bit careful. One of White's ideas is to play a reverse opening. If you brought your knight to f6 instead of c6, the position would be very much like the normal opening 1.e2-e4 e7-e5; 2.Ng1-f3 Nb8-c6, except that the colors are reversed and it would be White's turn to move. This can lead to a lot of sophisticated mind games, which as a beginner you shouldn't have to deal with.

Since as Black you almost always place your knight at c6 anyway, it makes sense to play that move. With a grip on the square at d4, White isn't likely to get the pawn to d4 quickly. Should White choose a plan involving the advance of the f-pawn, your bishop will take up a post at c5. Of course if White simply brings out the other knight, you do the same and you will have transferred the game to Four Knights territory.

3.f2-f4. On 3.Bf1-c4, just bring out the other knight, and the game will likely reach the Italian Four Knights after 3…Ng8-f6 4.Ng1-f3. If 4.d2-d3, consider the option of pinning the knight by playing 4…Bf8-b4. It is important to remember that the knight at c3 is a target for your pinning operation. You will see that in your main continuation too.

3...e5xf4; 4.Ng1-f3 Ng8-f6; 5.d2-d4 Bf8-b4.

The pin on the knight removes the defender of the pawn at e4. If White now captures your pawn at f4, you can take the pawn at e4 with your knight. In this case you may be able to pull off a little swindle. On **6.Bc1xf4 Nf6xe4; 7.Qd1-e2**, counter pinning your knight, you can just castle because if White captures the knight with the queen, you play your rook to e8.

7...O-O; 8.Qe2xe4 Rf8-e8.

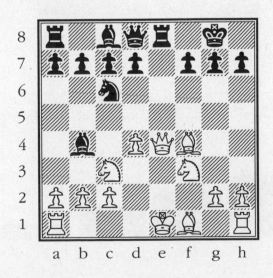

In order to save the queen, White must put the knight or the bishop at e5. You can attack with a pawn at d6 or f6 and the piece can't move away because it is pinned to the queen. So you will recover your sacrificed material, and enjoy the benefit of already being castled.

WHITE SMASHES OPEN THE CENTER

1.e2-e4	e7-e5
2.d2-d4	e5xd4

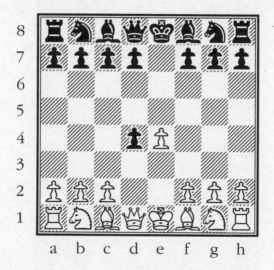

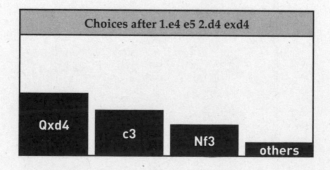

Choices after 1.e4 e5 2.d4 exd4

Qxd4 c3 Nf3 others

YOUR BLACK OPENINGS

Suppose your opponent is arrogant enough to try an immediate attempt to conquer the center? You take the pawn, of course. If White responds to your capture by recapturing with the queen, you will attack the queen with your knight, as you'll see in a moment. In later sections we will look at gambit approaches where White makes no effort to immediately recover the pawn. As you can see from the previous chart, the gambit approaches are as popular as the immediate capture.

3.Qd1xd4 Nb8-c6.

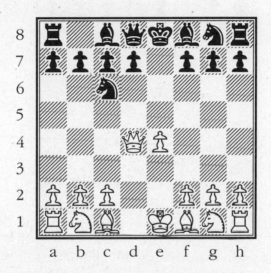

White must retreat the queen. If she goes to c3, you can pin and win by bringing your bishop to b4. Otherwise, just bring out the knight, then the bishop and castle. Don't waste a lot of time chasing the queen around. Concentrate on castling.

TWO-PAWN GAMBIT

1.e2-e4	e7-e5
2.d2-d4	e5xd4
3.c2-c3	

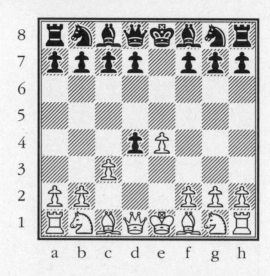

The Danish Gambit can be very dangerous if not handled properly. The same can't be said for White's other gambit approaches. If White brings out the knight from g1 to f3, then you are in the Scotch game after 3...Nb8-c6. When White brings the bishop out with 3.Bf1-c4, the same defense should lead you into the gambit variation of the Two Knights Defense. So the only gambit approach you need to be concerned with is the Danish.

3...d7-d5! This move takes all the fun out of the gambit. The ideas are the same as those of the Goering Gambit, which differs only in that White already has a knight at f3 and Black has a knight at c6 in that opening. You do not yet have knight at c6 in the present position, so White can capture the pawn at d4 with the queen.

4.Qd1xd4 d5xe4.

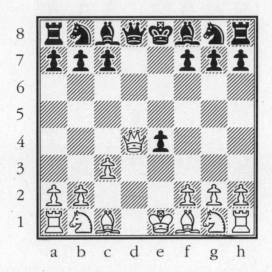

White can exchange queens, in which case your king will have to move and castling will no longer be an option. However you have an extra pawn, and with queens off the board, your king is quite safe in the middle of the board. So there is nothing to fear in that line.

On the other hand, should White capture the pawn at e4, giving check to your king, you can achieve the same exchange of queens by blocking with your queen. You can play more ambitiously by blocking with the bishop, so that you can then bring your knight out to f6 and castle. Your pieces will be in fighting position while the White queen is running around accomplishing nothing.

Since you don't usually allow positions where you are unable to castle, I will provide some specific advice about the position after 5.Qd4xd8+ Ke8xd8.

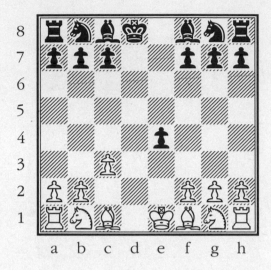

To keep your king safe, you will want to put your pawn at c6 and move the king to c7. White might be able to throw a monkey wrench into your plans by putting the bishop at f4, so before advancing your pawn to c6, you should move your bishop to d6 to take control of that line. In most gambits, I recommend a strategy to hand back the pawn. In this case, however, feel free to hold onto it by supporting it with a pawn at f5, a bishop at f5, or a knight at f6. Make your opponent work to recover the pawn, because if you can successfully hang onto it, you will likely win the game.

CLOSED GAMES

ON CLOSED GAMES

Most of your games will start with the advance of the king pawn. You are also likely to encounter games where White starts out by advancing the queen pawn to the center of the board. This leads to what is known as **a closed game**. The battles will wait until after both sides have their forces in place. You're not likely to run into other strategies too often, except perhaps for some pet-favorite moves.

At some point, however, you are almost certain to come face-to-face with the Queen's Gambit. As the quality of your opposition improves, you'll also run into a variety of attacking systems which are based on the advance of the d-pawn but do not involve the gambit. You may also run into some unfamiliar gambits and attacking formations. The following sections will show you how to handle them.

FIRST CHESS OPENINGS

1.d2-d4   **d7-d5**

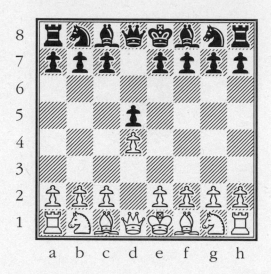

White isn't obliged to move the king pawn on the first move. There are nineteen alternatives, but for the most part none of the alternatives lead to as sharp a contest. Advancing the king pawn allows both the queen and a bishop into the game. Advancing the queen pawn really only allows the bishop at c1 to have a say, because the queen can't be of much help at d2 or d3.

Most players stick with moving the king pawn two squares forward until they have achieved a fairly high skill level. You will run into the other openings only rarely. Although the theory of those openings has been developed just as deeply and extensively as that of the king pawn games, there are far fewer tactical tricks, so we don't have to learn as much detail to be ready to meet them.

Your basic formation against all moves other than 1.e4 is to set up a solid defense and castle quickly. There isn't quite as much pressure to get the king out of the center because it is likely to remain closed for some time. Still, in order to complete the other tasks involving the rooks, you should try to castle in the first eight moves. Aim for the following formation.

CLOSED GAMES

What you do with your bishop at c8 depends on White's moves. If White exchanges a pawn for your pawn at d5—say by advancing the c-pawn or e-pawn—then you will recapture with your pawn at e6, and bring the bishop out along the diagonal that has opened up from c8 to h3. If not, the pawn at b6 steps forward one square and the bishop finds a home at b7.

We will now briefly look at all of the popular approaches for White in the closed games and flank games. Unless you regularly face opponents who choose moves other than 1.e2-e4, you do not have to study this material in depth. For the most part, you can simply aim for the formation presented above. In most cases it will not make much difference which order of moves is used.

The sections below should be studied as you need them. If all of your opponents start the game by moving the king pawn forward, you won't need this material at all. Eventually, however, you'll start to run into players who enjoy using some of the systems presented here.

After 1.d2-d4 d7-d5, White almost always plays either 2.c2-c4 or Ng1-f3 or occasionally 2.e2-e3, all other moves are very rare.

THE MAIN DEFENSE

1.d2-d4	d7-d5
2.c2-c4	e7-e6

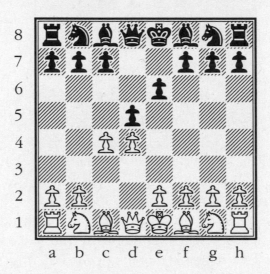

The **Queen's Gambit**, introduced when White serves up a pawn at c4 as a sacrificial offering, is one of the oldest and most respected openings. You should decline the offer, because if your d-pawn departs to the c-file, then White will be able to take complete control of the center. Black can get away with this at more advanced levels, but beginners should not concede the center without a fight.

After 2...e7-e6, Black has a solid center, but the bishop at c8 may have some difficulty getting into the game early. Solving this problem is really Black's only challenge in this opening. The solution I recommend is known as the **Tarrasch Defense.**

3.Nb1-c3. It doesn't matter which knight is brought out first. The plan remains the same. You challenge White's central pawn by bringing your pawn to c5.

3...c7-c5. If you look at the opening manuals, you'll find that in this position, White usually captures at d5. However, in amateur games, it is much more usual to see the pawn advance from e2 to e3.

CLOSED GAMES

The capture at d5 can be played at any time, but we'll look at it a little bit later on. Although it is the recommended move, many players don't like it because it removes the obstacle at e6 and allows the bishop at c8 to get into the game. Black pays a price for this, because there will be a weak pawn at d5. In the unlikely case that White follows the professional variation 4.c4xd5 e6xd5; 5.Ng1-f3 Nb8-c6; 6.g2-g3, the important thing to remember is that your bishop should go to e7 rather than d6.

The normal moves are 6...Ng8-f6; 7.Bf1-g2 Bf8-e7 and then both sides castle. I should point out, however, that none of my students have ever encountered this approach. On the other hand, almost all of my professional games have followed this variation.

Moving from professional concepts to the beginner arena, you should be aware that bringing out the knight with 4.Ng1-f3 is a mistake, because after 4...c5xd4; 5.Nf3xd4 e7-e5 White is already on the defensive.

4.e2-e3 Ng8-f6; 5.Ng1-f3 Nb8-c6.

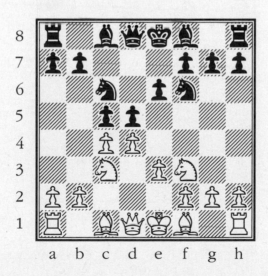

6.c4xd5. White can capture the pawn at c5 first, but it won't make any real difference.

6...e6xd5. If White does not capture the pawn at c5 now, you'll just bring your bishop out to d6 and then castle. It is better for White to delay the capture at c5, so that you have to waste a move with your bishop.

155

In a closed opening it isn't necessary to conserve time as much as it is in an open game, so the difference is not particularly important. Besides, White is running out of waiting moves. If White brings out the bishop from f1, where should it go? On the immediate 7.d4xc5 Bf8xc5, you are ready to castle and will be ahead of the game compared with the alternative bishop moves at the seventh turn. We'll look at moving the bishop to b5, since that pins the knight and has some impact on the game. Other moves are handled basically the same way.

7.Bf1-b5 Bf8-d6. A general rule in the Tarrasch Defense is that the bishop belongs at d6 unless White plays a pawn from g2 to g3, in which case the bishop should be at e7. Of course when White captures at c5, the bishop has to move again to capture the pawn at c5.

8.d4xc5 Bf8xc5.

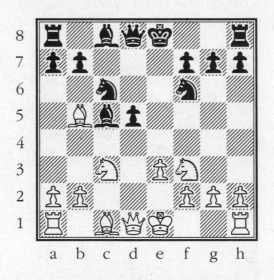

This is a typical Tarrasch position. Black enjoys freedom of movement, has as many pieces in the game as White does, and is ready to castle. In return for this wonderful position a small concession has to be made. The pawn at d5 is not very strong, however, it can be supported by a bishop at e6 if necessary. More ambitiously, Black can move the bishop to b4, pinning White's knight. In any case, it will be easy to complete the opening tasks by castling, connecting the rooks, and then moving at least one rook to the center. The next few moves will come naturally until you get to the point where the rooks are connected. Then you'll have to decide where to put them. There are three important central files: the d-file, e-file, and c-file. Determining the most effective positions for the rooks is not an easy task, and even top grandmasters sometimes stumble.

When the time comes, look at your opponent's pieces and try to figure out which two of those three files will most likely have an impact on the game, and place your rooks there. You can use your queen for the third file.

WHAT'S NEXT?

Now that you are familiar with the basic opening strategies you need to know, you should develop the other parts of your game. Then, after learning some strategy and tactics, and a bit about the endgame, you'll want to deepen your knowledge of opening strategies. However, you should concentrate on tactics for while.

In the opening phase of the game, you only need to know enough to escape the opening alive, with no weaknesses in your position. The four general guidelines presented in this book will be sufficient to solve most of the problems you will encounter at the chessboard. So don't spend a lot of time memorizing long variations. You are unlikely to run into the major opening variations used by professionals in your casual games.

Study of the endgame is very important, but unlikely to have much of an impact on your early games. You will not often reach positions with roughly equal material at the end of the game. In most cases you or your opponent will have a substantial advantage and no special technical skills will be required.

You will eventually need to deepen your understanding of openings, and may perhaps want to move on to more complicated strategies. Whether you prefer standard openings, exciting gambits, or the weird and wacky world of unorthodox openings, you can spend a lifetime exploring the possibilities.

AS WHITE

	1	2	3	4	5	6	7	8
1	e2-e4 e7-e5	Bf1-c4 Ng8-f6	Ng1-f3 Nb8-c6	Nf3-g5 d7-d5	e4xd5 Nf6xd5	Ng5xf7 Ke8xf7	Qd1-f3+ Kf7-e6	Nb1-c3
2	e2-e4 e7-e5	Bf1-c4 Ng8-f6	Ng1-f3 Nb8-c6	Nf3-g5 d7-d5	e4xd5 b7-b5	d5xc6 b5xc4	Qd1-e2	
3	e2-e4 e7-e5	Bf1-c4 Ng8-f6	Ng1-f3 Nb8-c6	Nf3-g5 d7-d5	e4xd5 Nc6-d4	d5-d6		
4	e2-e4 e7-e5	Bf1-c4 Ng8-f6	Ng1-f3 Nb8-c6	Nf3-g5 d7-d5	-- Nc6-a5	Bc4-b5+ c7-c6[2]	d5xc6 b7xc6	Qd1-f3
5	e2-e4 e7-e5	Bf1-c4 Ng8-f6	Ng1-f3 Nb8-c6	Nf3-g5 Bf8-c5	Bc4xf7+ Ke8-e7	Bf7-b3 Rh8-f8	O-O	
6	e2-e4 e7-e5	Bf1-c4 Ng8-f6	Ng1-f3 Nb8-c6	Nf3-g5 Nf6xe4	Bc4xf7+ Ke8-e7	d2-d3		
7	e2-e4 e7-e5	Bf1-c4 Ng8-f6	Ng1-f3 Nb8-c6	Nf3-g5 Qd8-e7	Bc4xf7+ Ke8-d8	Bf7-b3		
8	e2-e4 e7-e5	Bf1-c4 Ng8-f6	Ng1-f3 Nf6xe4	Nb1-c3 Ne4xc3	d2xc3 f7-f6	O-O Nb8-c6	Nf3-h4 g7-g6	Rf1-e1
9	e2-e4 e7-e5	Bf1-c4 Bf8-c5	Ng1-f3 Nb8-c6[3]	O-O Ng8-f6	d2-d3 h7-h6	c2-c3		
10	e2-e4 e7-e6	d2-d4 d7-d5	e4-e5 c7-c5	c2-c3 Nb8-c6	Ng1-f3 Qd8-b6	Bf1-d3 c5xd4	c3xd4 Bc8-d7	O-O
11	e2-e4 c7-c5	c2-c3 d7-d5	e4xd5 Qd8xd5	d2-d4 Ng8-f6	Ng1-f3 Bc8-g4	Bf1-e2 Nb8-c6	O-O c5xd4	c3xd4
12	e2-e4 c7-c6	d2-d4 d7-d5	e4-e5 Bc8-f5	Bf1-d3 Bf5xd3	Qd1xd3 e7-e6	Ng1-e2 c6-c5	c2-c3 Nb8-c6	O-O
13	e2-e4 g7-g6	d2-d4 Bf8-g7	c2-c3 d7-d6	Bf1-c4 Ng8-f6	Qd1-e2			
14	e2-e4 d7-d6	d2-d4 Ng8-f6	Bf1-c4 Nf6xe4	Bc4xf7+ Ke8xf7	Qd1-h5+ Kf7-e6	d4-d5+ Ke6-f6	Nb1-c3 Ne4xc3	Bc1-g5+
15	e2-e4 d7-d5	e4xd5 Qd8xd5	d2-d4 Ng8-f6	Ng1-f3 Bc8-g4	Bf1-e2 Nb8-c6	O-O Bg4xf3	Be2xf3 Qd5xd4	Bf3xc6+
16	e2-e4 Ng8-f6	Bf1-c4 Nf6xe4	Bc4xf7+ Ke8xf7	Qd1-h5+ Kf7-f6	Qh5-f3+ Kf6-e5	d2-d4+ Ke5xd4	Ng1-e2+ Kd4-e5	Bc1-f4+

AS BLACK

	1	2	3	4	5	6	7	8
1	e2-e4 e7-e5	Ng1-f3 Nb8-c6	Bf1-c4 Ng8-f6	Nf3-g5 d7-d5	e4xd5 Nc6-a5	Bc4-b5+ Bc8-d7	Qd1-e2 Bf8-d6	Nb1-c3 O-O
2	e2-e4 e7-e5	Ng1-f3 Nb8-c6	Bf1-c4 Ng8-f6	d2-d3 Bf8-e7				
3	e2-e4 e7-e5	Ng1-f3 Nb8-c6	Bf1-c4 Ng8-f6	d2-d4 e5xd4	e4-e5 Nf6-e4	O-O d7-d5	Bc4-b5 Bc8-d7	
4	e2-e4 e7-e5	Ng1-f3 Nb8-c6	Bf1-c4 Ng8-f6	O-O Nf6xe4	Nb1-c3 Ne4xc3	d2xc3 Bf8-e7		
5	e2-e4 e7-e5	Ng1-f3 Nb8-c6	Bf1-b5 Ng8-e7	O-O a7-a6	Bb5-a4 b7-b5	Ba4-b3 Ne7-g6	d2-d4 e5xd4	Nf3xd4 Nc6xd4
6	e2-e4 e7-e5	Ng1-f3 Nb8-c6	d2-d4 e5xd4	Nf3xd4 Bf8-c5	Nd4xc6 Qd8-f6	Qd1-d2 Qf6xc6		
7	e2-e4 e7-e5	Ng1-f3 Nb8-c6	Nb1-c3 Ng8-f6	Bf1-c4 Bf8-e7	O-O O-O	d2-d3 d7-d6		
8	e2-e4 e7-e5	Bf1-c4 Ng8-f6	d2-d3 Nb8-c6	f2-f4 Bf8-c5	Ng1-f3 d7-d6			
9	e2-e4 e7-e5	f2-f4 d7-d5	e4xd5 e5xf4	Ng1-f3 Bc8-g4	Bf1-b5+ c7-c6	d5xc6 b7xc6		
10	e2-e4 e7-e5	Nb1-c3 Nb8-c6	f2-f4 e5xf4	Ng1-f3 Ng8-f6	d2-d4 Bf8-b4	Bc1xf4 Nf6xe4	Qd1-e2 O-O	Qe2xe4 Rf8-e8
11	e2-e4 e7-e5	d2-d4 e5xd4	c2-c3 d7-d5	Qd1xd4 d5xe4	Qd4xd8+ Ke8xd8			
12	d2-d4 d7-d5	c2-c4[7] e7-e6	Nb1-c3 c7-c5	e2-e3 Ng8-f6	Ng1-f3 Nb8-c6	c4xd5 e6xd5	Bf1-b5 Bf8-d6	d4xc5 Bd6xc5
13	d2-d4 d7-d5	Ng1-f3 e7-e6	e2-e3 c7-c5	Bf1-d3 Ng8-f6	O-O Bf8-d6			
14	d2-d4 d7-d5	Ng1-f3 e7-e6	Bc1-f4 Bf8-d6	Bf4xd6 Qd8xf6				
15	d2-d4 d7-d5	Ng1-f3 e7-e6	Bc1-g5 Bf8-e7	Bg5xe7 Qd8xe7				
16	c2-c4 e7-e6	any d7-d5						